T0256114

Artificial Intelligence Hardware Design

Artificial Intelligence Hardware Design

Challenges and Solutions

Albert Chun Chen Liu and Oscar Ming Kin Law

Kneron Inc.,
San Diego, CA, USA

IEEE PRESS

WILEY

Published by John Wiley & Sons, Inc., Hoboken, New Jersey.
Published simultaneously in Canada.

For general information on our other products and services or for technical support, please contact our Customer Care Department within the United States at (800) 762-2974, outside the United States at (317) 572-3993 or fax (317) 572-4002.

Wiley also publishes its books in a variety of electronic formats. Some content that appears in print may not be available in electronic formats. For more information about Wiley products, visit our web site at www.wiley.com.

Library of Congress Cataloging-in-Publication data applied for:

ISBN: 9781119810452

Cover design by Wiley
Cover image: © Rasi Bhadramani/iStock/Getty Images

Set in 9.5/12.5pt STIXTwoText by Straive, Pondicherry, India

10 9 8 7 6 5 4 3 2 1

Contents

Author Biographies

Albert Chun Chen Liu is Kneron's founder and CEO. He is Adjunct Associate Professor at National Tsing Hua University, National Chiao Tung University, and National Cheng Kung University. After graduating from the Taiwan National Cheng Kung University, he got scholarships from Raytheon and the University of California to join the UC Berkeley/UCLA/UCSD research programs and then earned his Ph.D. in Electrical Engineering from the University of California Los Angeles (UCLA). Before establishing Kneron in San Diego in 2015, he worked in R&D and management positions in Qualcomm, Samsung Electronics R&D Center, MStar, and Wireless Information.

Albert has been invited to give lectures on computer vision technology and artificial intelligence at the University of California and be a technical reviewer for many internationally renowned academic journals. Also, Albert owned more than 30 international patents in artificial intelligence, computer vision, and image processing. He has published more than 70 papers. He is a recipient of the IBM Problem Solving Award based on the use of the EIP tool suite in 2007 and IEEE TCAS Darlington award in 2021.

Oscar Ming Kin Law developed his interest in smart robot development in 2014. He has successfully integrated deep learning with the self-driving car, smart drone, and robotic arm. He is currently working on humanoid development. He received a Ph.D. in Electrical and Computer Engineering from the University of Toronto, Canada.

Oscar currently works at Kneron for in-memory computing and smart robot development. He has worked at ATI Technologies, AMD, TSMC, and Qualcomm and led various groups for chip verification, standard cell design, signal integrity, power analysis, and Design for Manufacturability (DFM). He has conducted different seminars at the University of California, San Diego, University of Toronto, Qualcomm, and TSMC. He has also published over 60 patents in various areas.

Preface

With the breakthrough of the Convolutional Neural Network (CNN) for image classification in 2012, Deep Learning (DL) has successfully solved many complex problems and widely used in our everyday life, automotive, finance, retail, and healthcare. In 2016, Artificial Intelligence (AI) exceeded human intelligence that Google AlphaGo won the GO world championship through Reinforcement Learning (RL). AI revolution gradually changes our world, like a personal computer (1977), Internet (1994), and smartphone (2007). However, most of the efforts focus on software development rather than hardware challenges:

- Big input data
- Deep neural network
- Massive parallel processing
- Reconfigurable network
- Memory bottleneck
- Intensive computation
- Network pruning
- Data sparsity

This book shows how to resolve the hardware problems through various design ranging from CPU, GPU, TPU to NPU. Novel hardware can be evolved from those designs for further performance and power improvement:

- Parallel architecture
- Streaming Graph Theory
- Convolution optimization
- In-memory computation
- Near-memory architecture
- Network sparsity
- 3D neural processing

Organization of the Book

Chapter 1 introduces neural network and discusses neural network development history.

Chapter 2 reviews Convolutional Neural Network (CNN) model and describes each layer functions and examples.

Chapter 3 lists out several parallel architectures, Intel CPU, Nvidia GPU, Google TPU, and Microsoft NPU. It emphasizes hardware/software integration for performance improvement. Nvidia Deep Learning Accelerator (NVDLA) opensource project is chosen for FPGA hardware implementation.

Chapter 4 introduces a streaming graph for massive parallel computation through Blaize GSP and Graphcore IPU. They apply the Depth First Search (DFS) for task allocation and Bulk Synchronous Parallel Model (BSP) for parallel operations.

Chapter 5 shows how to optimize convolution with the University of California, Los Angeles (UCLA) Deep Convolutional Neural Network (DCNN) accelerator filter decomposition and Massachusetts Institute of Technology (MIT) Eyeriss accelerator Row Stationary dataflow.

Chapter 6 illustrates in-memory computation through Georgia Institute of Technologies Neurocube and Stanford Tetris accelerator using Hybrid Memory Cube (HMC) as well as University of Bologna Neurostream accelerator using Smart Memory Cubes (SMC).

Chapter 7 highlights near-memory architecture through the Institute of Computing Technology (ICT), Chinese Academy of Science, DaDianNao supercomputer and University of Toronto Cnvlutin accelerator. It also shows Cnvlutin how to avoid ineffectual zero operations.

Chapter 8 chooses Stanford Energy Efficient Inference Engine, Institute of Computing Technology (ICT), Chinese Academy of Science Cambricon-X, Massachusetts Institute of Technology (MIT) SCNN processor and Microsoft SeerNet accelerator to handle network sparsity.

Chapter 9 introduces an innovative 3D neural processing with a network bridge to overcome power and thermal challenges. It also solves the memory bottleneck and handles the large neural network processing.

In English edition, several chapters are rewritten with more detailed descriptions. New deep learning hardware architectures are also included. Exercises challenge the reader to solve the problems beyond the scope of this book. The instructional slides are available upon request.

We shall continue to explore different deep learning hardware architectures (i.e. Reinforcement Learning) and work on a in-memory computing architecture with new high-speed arithmetic approach. Compared with the Google Brain floating-point (BFP16) format, the new approach offers a wider dynamic range, higher performance, and less power dissipation. It will be included in a future revision.

Albert Chun Chen Liu
Oscar Ming Kin Law

Acknowledgments

First, we would like to thank all who have supported the publication of the book. We are thankful to Iain Law and Enoch Law for the manuscript preparation and project development. We would like to thank Lincoln Lee and Amelia Leung for reviewing the content. We also thank Claire Chang, Charlene Jin, and Alex Liao for managing the book production and publication. In addition, we are grateful to the readers of the Chinese edition for their valuable feedback on improving the content of this book. Finally, we would like to thank our families for their support throughout the publication of this book.

Albert Chun Chen Liu
Oscar Ming Kin Law

Table of Figures

1

Introduction

With the advancement of Deep Learning (DL) for image classification in 2012 [1], Convolutional Neural Network (CNN) extracted the image features and successfully classified the objects. It reduced the error rate by 10% compared with the traditional computer vision algorithmic approaches. Finally, ResNet showed the error rate better than human 5% accuracy in 2015. Different Deep Neural Network (DNN) models are developed for various applications ranging from automotive, finance, retail to healthcare. They have successfully solved complex problems and widely used in our everyday life. For example, Tesla autopilot guides the driver for lane changes, navigating interchanges, and highway exit. It will support traffic sign recognition and city automatic driving in near future.

In 2016, Google AlphaGo won the GO world championship through Reinforcement Learning (RL) [2]. It evaluated the environment, decided the action, and, finally, won the game. RL has large impacts on robot development because the robot adapts to the changes in the environment through learning rather than programming. It expands the robot role in industrial automation. The Artificial Intelligent (AI) revolution has gradually changed our world, like a personal computer (1977)[1], the Internet (1994)[2] and smartphone (2007).[3] It significantly improves the human living (Figure 1.1).

---

1 Apple IIe (1997) and IBM PC (1981) provided the affordable hardware for software development, new software highly improved the working efficiency in our everyday life and changed our world.
2 The information superhighway (1994) connects the whole world through the Internet that improves personal-to-personal communication. Google search engine makes the information available at your fingertips.
3 Apple iPhone (2007) changed the phone to the multimedia platform. It not only allows people to listen to the music and watch the video, but also integrates many utilities (i.e. e-mail, calendar, wallet, and note) into the phone.

Artificial Intelligence Hardware Design: Challenges and Solutions, First Edition.
Albert Chun Chen Liu and Oscar Ming Kin Law.
© 2021 The Institute of Electrical and Electronics Engineers, Inc. Published 2021 by John Wiley & Sons, Inc.

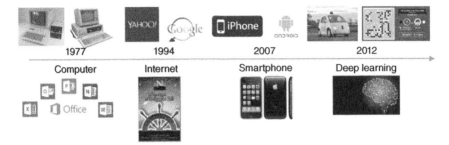

Figure 1.1 High-tech revolution.

1.1 Development History

Neural Network [3] had been developed for a long time. In 1943, the first computer Electronic Numerical Integrator and Calculator (ENIAC) was constructed at the University of Pennsylvania. At the same time, a neurophysiologist, Warren McCulloch, and a mathematician, Walter Pitts, described how neurons might work [4] and modeled a simple neural network using an electrical circuit. In 1949, Donald Hebb wrote the book, The Organization of Behavior, which pointed out how the neural network is strengthened through practice (Figure 1.2).

In the 1950s, Nathanial Rochester simulated the first neural network in IBM Research Laboratory. In 1956, the Dartmouth Summer Research Project on Artificial Intelligence linked up artificial intelligence (AI) with neural network for joint project development. In the following year, John von Neumann suggested to implement simple neuron functions using telegraph relays or vacuum tubes. Also,

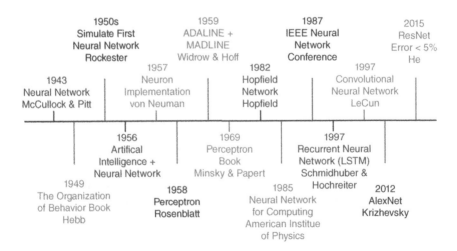

Figure 1.2 Neural network development timeline.

a neurobiologist from Cornell University, Frank Rosenblatt, worked on Perceptron [5], which is a single-layer perceptron to classify the results from two classes. The perception computes the weighted sum of the inputs and subtracts a threshold, and then outputs one of two possible results. Perception is the oldest neural network model still used today. However, Marvin Minsky and Seymour Papert published the book, Perceptron [6], to show the limitation of perception in 1969.

In 1959, Bernard Widrow and Marcian Hoff from Stanford University developed Multiple ADaptive LINear Elements called ADALINE and MADALINE, which were adaptive filter to eliminate the echoes in the phone line. Due to unmatured electronics and fear the machine impacts toward humans, neural network development was halted for a decade.

Until 1982, John Hopfield presented a new neural network model, the Hopfield neural network [7], with the mathematical analysis in the National Academy of Sciences. At the same time, the United States started to fund neural network research to compete with Japan after Japan announced fifth-generation AI research in the US-Japan Cooperative/Competitive Neural Networks' joint conference. In 1985, the American Institute of Physics started the annual meeting, Neural Network for Computing. By 1987, the first IEEE neural network international conference took place with 1800 attendees. In 1997, Schmidhuber and Hochreiter proposed a recurrent neural network model with Long-Short Term Memory (LSTM) useful for future time series speech processing. In 1997, Yann LeCun published Gradient-Based Learning Applied to Document Recognition [8]. It introduced the CNN that laid the foundation for modern DNN development (Figure 1.3).

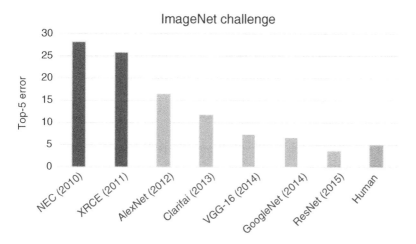

Figure 1.3 ImageNet challenge.

During ImageNet Large Scale Visual Recognition Challenge (ILSVRC 2012) [9], University of Toronto researchers applied CNN Model, AlexNet [1], successfully recognized the object and achieved a top-5 error rate 10% better than traditional computer vision algorithmic approaches. For ILSVRC, there are over 14 million images with 21 thousand classes and more than 1 million images with bounding box. The competition focused on 1000 classes with a trimmed database for image classification and object detection. For image classification, the class label is assigned to the object in the images and it localizes the object with a bounding box for object detection. With the evolution of DNN models, Clarifia [10], VGG-16 [11], and GoogleNet [12], the error rate was rapidly reduced. In 2015, ResNet [13] showed an error rate of less than 5% of human level accuracy. The rapid growth of deep learning is transforming our world.

1.2 Neural Network Models

The brain consists of 86 billion neurons and each neuron has a cell body (or soma) to control the function of the neuron. Dendrites are the branch-like structures extending away from the cell body responsible for neuron communication. It receives the message from other neurons and allows the message to travel to the cell body. An axon carries an electric impulse from the cell body to the opposite end of the neuron, an axon terminal that passes the impulse to another neuron. The synapse is the chemical junction between the axon terminal of one neuron and dendrite where the chemical reaction occurs, excited and inhibited. It decides how to transmit the message between the neurons. The structure of a neuron allows the brain to transmit the message to the rest of the body and control all the actions (Figure 1.4).

The neural network model is derived from a human neuron. It consists of the node, weight, and interconnect. The node (cell body) controls the neural network operation and performs the computation. The weight (axon) connects to either a single node or multiple ones for signal transfer. The activation (synapse) decides the signal transfer from one node to others.

1.3 Neural Network Classification

The neural network models are divided into supervised, semi-supervised, and unsupervised learning.

1.3.1 Supervised Learning

Supervised learning sets the desired output and trains with a particular input dataset to minimize the error between the desired and predicted outputs. After the

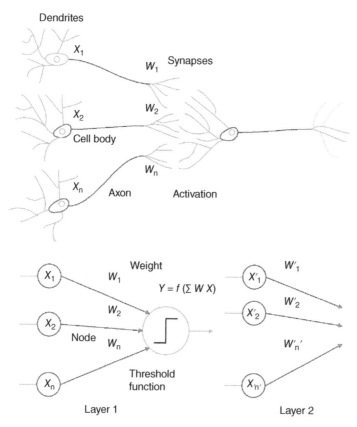

Figure 1.4 Neural network model.

successful training, the network predicts the outputs based on unknown inputs. The popular supervised models are CNN and Recurrent Neural Network (RNN) including Long Short-Term Memory Network (LSTM).

Regression is typically used for supervised learning; it predicts the value based on the input dataset and finds the relationship between the input and output. Linear regression is the popular regression approach (Figure 1.5).

1.3.2 Semi-supervised Learning

Semi-supervised learning is based on partial labeled output for training where Reinforcement Learning (RL) is the best example. Unlabeled data is mixed with a small amount of labeled data that can improve learning accuracy under a different environment.

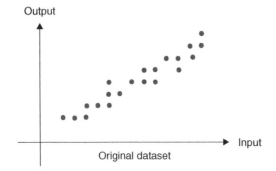

Figure 1.5 Regression.

Output

Input

Original dataset

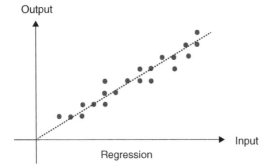

Output

Input

Regression

1.3.3 Unsupervised Learning

Unsupervised learning is the network that learns the important features from the dataset which exploits the relationship among the inputs through clustering, dimensionality reduction, and generative techniques. The examples include Auto Encoder (AE), Restricted Boltzmann Machine (RBM), and Deep Belief Network (DBN).

Clustering is a useful technique for unsupervised learning. It divides the dataset into multiple groups where the data points are similar to each other in the same group. The popular clustering algorithm is k-means technique (Figure 1.6).

1.4 Neural Network Framework

The software frameworks are developed to support deep learning applications. The most popular academic framework is Caffe which is migrated into Pytorch. Pytorch is a deep learning research platform that provides maximum flexibility and speed. It replaces NumPy package to fully utilize GPU computational resource. TensorFlow is a dataflow symbolic library used for industrial

Figure 1.6 Clustering.

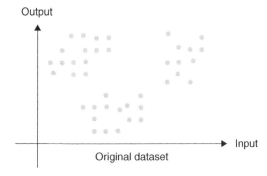

Output

Input

Original dataset

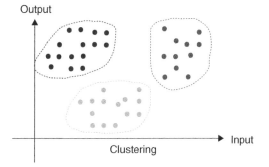

Output

Input

Clustering

applications supported by many companies (such as Intel, AMD, and Qualcomm, etc.). It runs on different platforms including CPU, GPU, and TPU with multiple language supports, Python, C++, Java, JavaScript, GO as well as third-party package, C#, MATLAB, Julia, Scala, Rust OCaul, and Crystal. TensorFlow can be used for both training and inference. Keras is a user-friendly, modular, and extensible package with TensorFlow, Theano, and Microsoft Cognitive Toolkits as backend tools. It is easy to develop deep learning applications. MATLAB is a numerical computational toolkit; it not only supports deep learning but also different applications. It can act as a client-server to integrate deep learning into STEM educational platform, LEGO Mindstorm EV3,[4] and Vex robotics (Table 1.1).

The framework supports both training and inference:

- Training feeds the dataset into the network where the network parameters are updated to minimize the error between the desired and predicted outputs. The training is compute-intensive with floating-point arithmetic to enhance the

---

4 Iain Law, Enoch Law and Oscar Law, LEGO Smart AI Robot, https://www.youtube.com/watch?v=NDnVtFx-rkM.

Table 1.1 Neural network framework.

Software	Developer	Release	Platform	Interface
TensorFlow[a]	Google Brian Team	2015	Linux, macOS, Windows	Python, C++
Caffe[b]	Berkeley Vision and Learning Center	2013	Linux, macOS, Windows	Python, C++, Matlab
Microsoft Cognitive Toolkit[c]	Microsoft	2016	Linux, Windows	Python (Keras), C++, BrainScript
Torch[d]	Ronan Collobert, Koray Kavukcuoglu, Clement Farabet	2002	Linux, macOS, Windows, iOS, Android	Lua, LuaJIT, C, C++
PyTorch[e]	Adam Paszke, Sam Gross, Soumith Chintala, Gregory Chanan	2016	Linux, macOS, Windows	Python, C, C++, CUDA
MXNet[f]	Apache Software Foundation	2015	Linux, macOS, Windows, AWS, iOS, Android	Python, C++, Julia, Matlab, Javascript, Go, R, Scala, Perl, Clojure
Chainer[g]	Preferred Networks	2015	Linux, macOS	Python
Keras[h]	Francois Chollet	2015	Linux, macOS, Windows	Python, R
Deeplearning4j[i]	Skymind Engineering Team	2014	Linux, macOS, Windows, Android	Python(Keras), Java, Scala, Clojure, Kotlin
Matlab[j]	MathWorks		Linux, macOS, Windows	C, C++, Java, Matlab

[a] http://www.tensorflow.org.
[b] http://caffe.berkeleyvision.org.
[c] http://github.com/Microsoft/CNTK.
[d] http://torch.ch.
[e] http://pytorch.org.
[f] https://mxnet.apache.org.
[g] http://chainer.org.
[h] http://keras.io.
[i] http://deeplearning4j.org.
[j] http://mathworks.com.

accuracy. It takes few hours to few days to train the network using cloud computing or High-Performance Computing (HPC) processor.

- The inference predicts the output through a trained neural network model. It only takes few seconds to a minute to predict the output using fixed-point format. Most of the deep learning accelerators are optimized for inference through pruning network and network sparsity using quantization.
- All the popular Neural Network frameworks support NVIDIA Compute Unified Device Architecture (CUDA) which fully utilize the powerful GPU to perform the parallel computation.

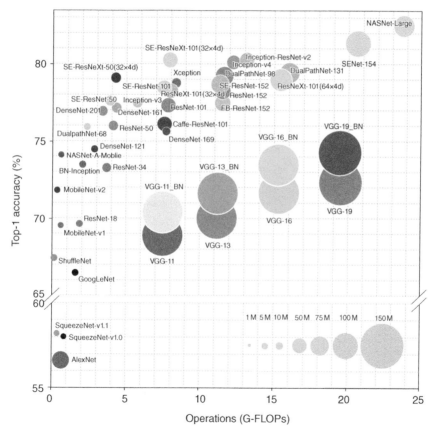

Figure 1.7 Neural network top 1 accuracy vs. computational complexity.

1.5   Neural Network Comparison

After the AlexNet [1] is emerged in 2012, various neural network models are developed. The models become larger, deeper, and more complex. They all demand intensive computation and high memory bandwidth. Different neural network models are compared [14, 15] in terms of computational complexity, model efficiency, and memory utilization (Figures 1.7–1.9).

To improve computational efficiency, new deep learning hardware architectures are developed to support intensive computation and high-memory bandwidth demands. To understand the deep learning accelerator requirements, CNN is introduced in the next chapter. It highlights the design challenges and discusses the hardware solutions.

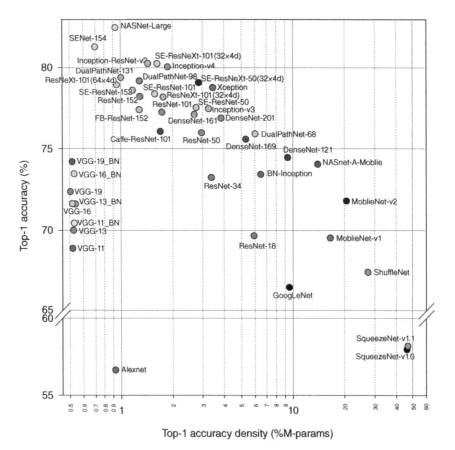

Figure 1.8   Neural network top 1 accuracy density vs. model efficiency [14].

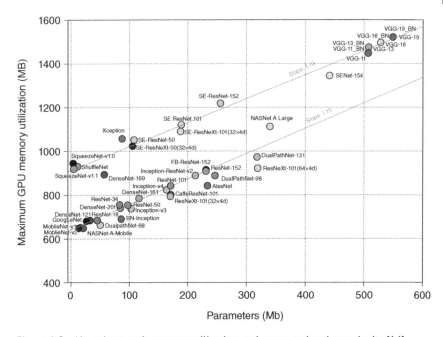

Figure 1.9   Neural network memory utilization and computational complexity [14].

Exercise

1   Why is the deep learning approach better than the algorithmic one?

2   How does deep learning impact the automotive, finance, retail, and health-care industries?

3   How will deep learning affect the job market in the next ten years?

4   What have changes of the neural networks, AlexNet, Clarifai, VGG-16, GoogleNet, and ResNet made it better than human image classification?

5   What is the fundamental difference between Convolutional Neural Network and Reinforcement Learning?

6   Why do people fear the rise of a machine?

7   What are the different requirements for training and inference?

8 Why do people need deep learning hardware?

9 What is the future direction of deep learning development?

References

1 Krizhevsky, A., Sutskever, I., and Hinton, G.E. (2012). *ImageNet Classification with Deep Convolutional Neural Network. NIPS.*

2 Silver, D., Huang, A., Maddison, C.J. et al. (2016). Mastering the game of go with deep neural networks and tree search. *Nature*: 484–489.

3 Strachnyi, K. (2019). Brief History of Neural Networks Analytics Vidhya, 23 January 2019 [Online].

4 McCulloch, W.S. and Pitts, W.H. (1943). A logical calculus of the ideas immanent in nervous activity. *The Bulletin of Mathematical Biophysics* 5 (4): 115–133.

5 Rosenblatt, F. (1958). The perceptron – a probabilistic model for information storage and organization in the brain. *Psychological Review* 65 (6): 386–408.

6 Minsky, M.L. and Papert, S.A. (1969). *Perceptrons.* MIT Press.

7 Hopfield, J.J. (1982). Neural networks and physical systems with emergent collective computational abilities. *Proceeding of National Academy of Sciences* 79: 2554–2558.

8 LeCun, Y., Bottou, L., and Haffnrt, P. (1998). Gradient-based learning applied to document recognition. *Proceedings of the IEEE* 86 (11): 2278–2324.

9 Russakobsky, O., Deng, J., and Su, H., et al. (2015). ImageNet Large Scale Visual Recognition Challenge. arXiv:1409.0575v3.

10 Howard, A.G. (2013). Some Improvements on Deep Convolutional Neural Network Based Image Classification. arXiv:1312.5402v1.

11 Simonyan, K. and Zisserman, A. (2014). Very Deep Convolutional Networks for Large-Scale Image Recognition. arXiv:14091556v6.

12 Szegedy, C., Liu, W., Jia, Y., et al. (2015). Going deeper with convolutions. *IEEE Conference on Computer Vision and Pattern Recognition (CVPR)*, 1–9.

13 He, K., Zhang, X., Ren, S., and Sun, J. (2016). Deep residual learning for image recognition. *IEEE Conference on Computer Vision and Pattern Recognition (CVPR)*, 770–778.

14 Bianco, S., Cadene, R., Celona, L., and Napoletano, P. (2018). Benchmark Analysis of Representative Deep Neural Network Architecture. arXiv:1810.00736v2.

15 Canziani, A., Culurciello, E., and Paszke, A. (2017). An Analysis of Deep Neural Network Models for Practical Applications. arXiv:1605.07678v4.

2

Deep Learning

The classical Deep Neural Network (DNN), AlexNet[1] [1] is derived from LeNet [2] with wider and deeper layers. It consists of eight layers: the first five layers are the convolutional layer with the nonlinear activation layer, Rectified Linear Unit (ReLU). It is followed by the max-pooling layer to reduce the kernel size and the Local Response Normalization (LRN) layer to improve the computation stability (Figure 2.1). The last three layers are fully connected layers for object classification (Figure 2.2).

Why does AlexNet show better image classification than LeNet? The deeper DNN model allows the feature maps [3] evolved from the simple feature maps to the complete ones. Therefore, the deeper DNN model achieves better top 1 accuracy during ILVSRC competition. The major drawback of the DNN model is intensive computation [4] and high memory bandwidth demands. The convolution requires 1.1 billion computations that occupy about 90% of computational resources (Figure 2.3).

2.1 Neural Network Layer

In this section, it briefly discusses the general neural network layer functions [5–8]. It includes convolutional layer, activation layer, pooling layer, batch normalization, dropout, and fully connected layer.

2.1.1 Convolutional Layer

The convolutional layer targets for feature extraction. The input feature maps (ifmaps) convolve with the stacked filter weights (fmaps) to extract the object features across all the channels. Multiple input feature maps can be processed

---

1 AlexNet image input size should be $227 \times 227 \times 3$ rather than $224 \times 224 \times 3$ typo in original paper.

Artificial Intelligence Hardware Design: Challenges and Solutions, First Edition.
Albert Chun Chen Liu and Oscar Ming Kin Law.
© 2021 The Institute of Electrical and Electronics Engineers, Inc. Published 2021
by John Wiley & Sons, Inc.

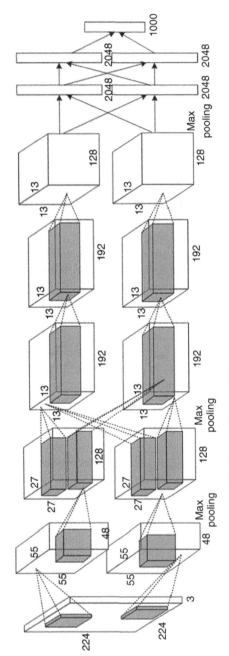

Figure 2.1 Deep neural network AlexNet architecture [1].

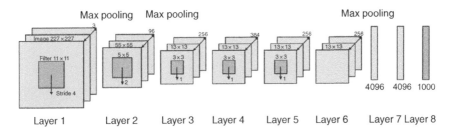

Figure 2.2 Deep neural network AlexNet model parameters.

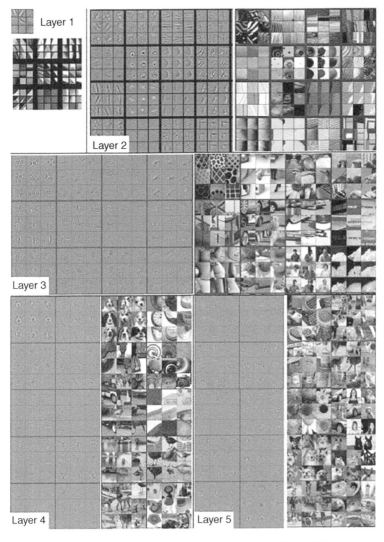

Figure 2.3 Deep neural network AlexNet feature map evolution [3].

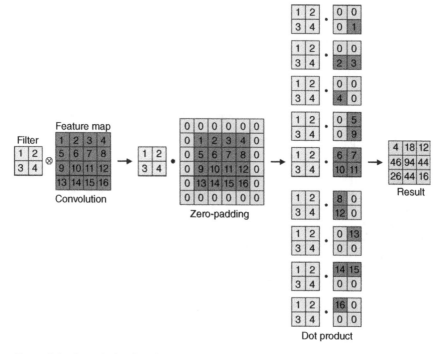

Figure 2.4 Convolution function.

together as a batch to improve the filter weights' reuse. The output is called output feature maps (ofmaps). For some network models, an additional bias offset is introduced. The zero-padding is used for edge filtering without the feature size reduction (Figure 2.4). The stride is designed for a sliding window to avoid the large output. The convolution is defined as

$$Y = X \otimes W \tag{2.1}$$

$$y_{i,j,k} = \sum_{k=0}^{K-1}\sum_{m=0}^{M-1}\sum_{n=0}^{N-1} x_{si+m,sj+n,k} \times w_{m,n,k} + \beta_{i,j,k} \tag{2.2}$$

$$W' = \frac{\left(W - M + 2P\right)}{S} + 1 \tag{2.3}$$

$$H' = \frac{\left(H - N + 2P\right)}{S} + 1 \tag{2.4}$$

$$D' = K \tag{2.5}$$

where

$y_{i,j,k}$ is the output feature maps, width W', height H', depth D' at i, j, with kth filter

$x_{m,n,k}$ is the input feature maps, width W, height H, depth D at m, n with kth filter

$w_{m,n}$ is the kth stacked filter weights with kernel size M (vertical) and N (horizontal)

β is the learning bias with n bias

P is the zero-padding size

S is the stride size

2.1.2 Activation Layer

A nonlinear activation layer (also called threshold function) is applied after the convolutional or fully connected layer. It rectifies the negative convolutional results (the extracted features do not exist) and introduces the network sparsity. There are various nonlinear activation functions and ReLU is the most popular one.

- Sigmoid compresses the output range between 0 and 1 like synapse inhibited and excited
- Hyperbolic tangent is similar to sigmoid with a range between –1 and 1. It is zero-centered to avoid the bias shift
- Rectified Linear Unit (ReLU) zeros the negative output to make the network robust to noise. It simplifies the hardware implementation through sign determination but introduces sparsity to the network
- Leaky Rectified Linear Unit is equivalent to maxout unit
- Exponential Linear Unit offers additional parameters and adjusts the output around zero (Figure 2.5)

$$Sigmoid\ Y = \frac{1}{1 + e^{-x}} \tag{2.6}$$

$$Hyperbolic\ tangent\ Y = \frac{e^x - e^{-x}}{e^x + e^{-x}} \tag{2.7}$$

$$Rectified\ linear\ unit\ Y = max(0, x) \tag{2.8}$$

$$Leaky\ rectified\ linear\ unit\ Y = max(\alpha x, x) \tag{2.9}$$

$$Exponential\ linear\ unit\ Y = \begin{cases} x & x \geq 0 \\ \alpha\left(e^x - 1\right) & x < 0 \end{cases} \tag{2.10}$$

where

Y is the activation output

X is the activation input

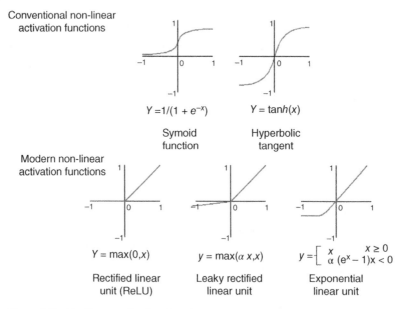

Conventional non-linear activation functions

$Y = 1/(1 + e^{-x})$

$Y = \tanh(x)$

Symoid function

Hyperbolic tangent

Modern non-linear activation functions

$Y = \max(0,x)$

$y = \max(\alpha x, x)$

$y = \begin{cases} x & x \geq 0 \\ \alpha(e^x - 1) & x < 0 \end{cases}$

Rectified linear unit (ReLU)

Leaky rectified linear unit

Exponential linear unit

Figure 2.5 Nonlinear activation functions.

2.1.3 Pooling Layer

Pooling is used to reduce the feature maps dimension; the network becomes more robust and invariant to the small shifts and distortions. The pooling is further divided into the maximum and average pooling. The maximum is preferred over the average one because it distinguishes the small features in the input feature maps (Figure 2.6).

$$Max\ pooling\ y_{i,j,k} = max_{m,n \in R_{M,N}}\left(x_{m,n,k}\right) \tag{2.11}$$

$$Average\ pooling\ y_{i,j,k} = \frac{1}{(M \times N)}\sum_{m}^{M-1}\sum_{n}^{N-1}x_{si+m,sj+n,k} \tag{2.12}$$

$$W' = \frac{W - M}{S} + 1 \tag{2.13}$$

$$H' = \frac{H - N}{S} + 1 \tag{2.14}$$

where

$y_{i,j,k}$ is the pooling output at position i, j, k with width W' and height H'

$x_{m,n,k}$ is the pooling input at position m, n, k with width W and height H

M, N are the pooling size with width M and height N

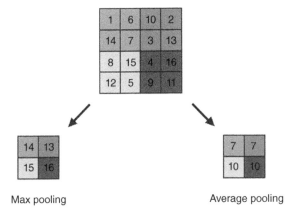

Max pooling   Average pooling

Figure 2.6 Pooling functions.

2.1.4 Normalization Layer

For deep learning, the layer output feeds to the next layer input which affects the data distribution for covariance shift and causally relates with the prediction accuracy. Batch normalization controls the input distortion with zero mean and unit standard deviation. It makes the network more robust to the weight initialization and the covariance shift through normalizing and scaling. It speeds up the training with higher accuracy. Currently, the Batch Normalization (BN) replaces the Local Response Normalization (LRN) where the normalization can be further scaled and shifted.

Local Response Normalization

$$b_{x,y}^i = \frac{a_{x,y}^i}{\left(k + \sum_{j=max\left(0, i-\frac{n}{2}\right)}^{min\left(N-1, i+\frac{n}{2}\right)} \left(a_{x,y}^i\right)^2\right)^\beta} \tag{2.15}$$

where

$b_{x,y}^i$ is the normalization output at location x, y

$a_{x,y}^i$ is the normalization input at location x, y

α is the normalization constant

β is the contrast constant

k is used to avoid singularities

N is the number of channels

Batch Normalization

$$y_i = \frac{x_i - \mu}{\sqrt[2]{\sigma^2 + \varepsilon}} \gamma + \alpha \qquad (2.16)$$

$$\mu = \frac{1}{n} \sum_{i=0}^{n-1} x_i \qquad (2.17)$$

$$\sigma^2 = \frac{1}{n} \sum_{i=0}^{n-1} (x_i - \mu)^2 \qquad (2.18)$$

where
Y_i is the output of Batch Normalization with depth n
X_i is the input of Batch Normalization with depth n
μ and σ are the statistical parameters collected during training
α, ε and Υ are training hyper-parameters

2.1.5 Dropout Layer

During the training, the dropout layer randomly ignores the activation to prevent overfitting through reducing the neuron correlation (Figure 2.7).

2.1.6 Fully Connected Layer

The fully connected layer is used for object classification. It can be viewed as the convolutional layer with no weight sharing and reuse convolutional layer for computation.

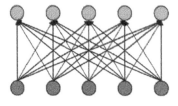
Original layer

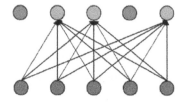
Dropout layer

Figure 2.7 Dropout layer.

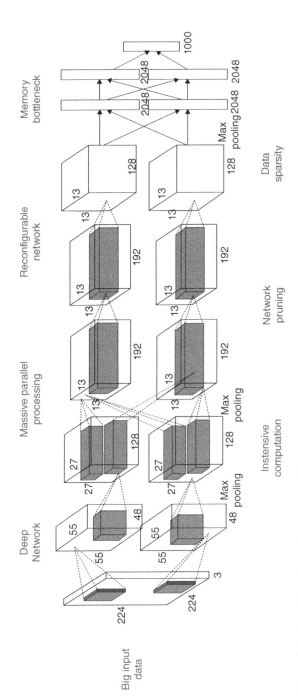

Figure 2.8 Deep learning hardware issues [1].

$$y_i = \sum_{m=0}^{M-1}\sum_{n=0}^{N-1} w_{i,m,n} x_{m,n} \qquad (2.19)$$

where

y_i is the fully connected output at position i

$x_{m,n}$ is the fully connected layer input with width M and height N

$w_{i,m,n}$ is the connected weight between output y_i and input $x_{m,n}$

2.2 Deep Learning Challenges

- Big Input Data: For AlexNet, the $227 \times 227 \times 3$ pixels input image convolves with 96 filters with weights $11 \times 11 \times 3$ and a stride of 4 pixels for the first convolutional layer. It imposes an intense computational requirement. The high-quality image further increases the loading for deep learning processing (Figure 2.8).
- Deep Network: AlexNet consists of eight layers. The depth of the model is increased dramatically (i.e. ResNet-152 has 152 layers). It increases the training time from hours to days as well as the inference response.
- Massive Parallel Processing: The convolution occupies over 90% of computational resource;[2] the massively parallel architecture is required to speed up the overall computation. The traditional central processing unit (CPU) is no longer to handle such requirements.
- Reconfigurable Network: The evolution of deep learning requires a reconfigurable network to fulfill different model demands.
- Memory Bottleneck: The high memory access becomes the deep learning challenge. Various memory schemes are developed to resolve this issue.
- Intensive Computation: The deep learning hardware applies floating-point arithmetic for training and inference. It requires complex hardware to process the data with long runtime. It demands a better scheme to speed up the computation.
- Network Pruning: Many filter weights have zero or near-zero value. Network pruning is required to eliminate the unused connections for a more effective network structure.
- Data Sparsity: The deep learning accelerator must ignore the ineffectual zero in order to improve the overall performance.

Exercise

1 Why does the deep learning model often employ a convolutional layer?

2 What is the best filter size for convolution?

---

2 AlexNet neural network model in Table 2.1.

Table 2.1 AlexNet neural network model.

Layer	Size	Filter	Depth	Stride	Padding	Number of parameters	Forward computation
Conv1 + ReLu	$3 \times 227 \times 227$	11×11	96	4		$(11 \times 11 \times 3 + 1) \times 96 = 34\,944$	$(11 \times 11 \times 3 + 1) \times 96 \times 55 \times 55 = 105\,705\,600$
Max pooling	$96 \times 55 \times 55$	3×3		2			
Norm	$96 \times 27 \times 27$						
Conv2 + ReLu		5×5	256	1	2	$(5 \times 5 \times 96 + 1) \times 256 = 614\,656$	$(5 \times 5 \times 96 + 1) \times 256 \times 27 \times 27 = 448\,084\,224$
Max pooling	$256 \times 27 \times 27$	3×3		2			
Norm	$256 \times 13 \times 13$						
Conv3 + ReLu		3×3	384	1	1	$(3 \times 3 \times 256 \times 1) \times 384 = 885\,120$	$(3 \times 3 \times 256 \times 1) \times 384 \times 13 \times 13 = 14\,958\,280$
Conv4 + ReLu	$384 \times 13 \times 13$	3×3	384	1	1	$(3 \times 3 \times 384 + 1) \times 384 = 1\,327\,488$	$(3 \times 3 \times 384 + 1) \times 384 \times 13 \times 13 = 224\,345\,472$
Conv5 + ReLu	$384 \times 13 \times 13$	3×3	256	1	1	$(3 \times 3 \times 384 + 1) \times 256 = 884\,992$	$(3 \times 3 \times 384 + 1) \times 256 \times 13 \times 13 = 149\,563\,648$
Max pooling	$256 \times 13 \times 13$	3×3		2			
Dropout (rate 0.5)	$256 \times 6 \times 6$						
FC6 + ReLu						$256 \times 6 \times 6 = 37\,748\,736$	$256 \times 6 \times 6 \times 4096 = 37\,748\,736$
Dropout (rate 0.5)	4096						
FC7 + ReLu						$4096 \times 4096 = 16\,777\,216$	$4096 \times 4096 = 16\,777\,216$
FC8 + ReLu	4096					$4096 \times 1000 = 4\,096\,000$	$4096 \times 1000 = 4\,096\,000$
1000 classes							
Overall						$62\,369\,152 = 62.3$ million	$1\,135\,906\,176 = 1.1$ billion
						Conv: 3.7 million (6%)	Conv: 1.08 billion (95%)
						FC: 58.6 million (94%)	FC: 58.6 million (5%)

3 Why is the floating-point computation so expensive?

4 What is the function of zero-padding?

5 What is the purpose of the sliding window (stride)?

6 How does the nonlinear activation function work?

7 What is the drawback of Rectified Linear Unit (ReLU)?

8 Why is maximum pooling preferred over average pooling?

9 What is the difference between Batch Normalization approach and Local Response Normalization approach?

10 How can the convolutional layer be modified for the fully connected one?

References

1 Krizhevsky, A., Sutskever, I., and Hinton, G.E. (2012). *ImageNet Classification with Deep Convolutional Neural Network. NIPS.*

2 LeCun, Y., Kavukcuoglu, K., and Farabet, C. (2010). Convolutional networks and applications in vision. *Proceedings of 2010 IEEE International Symposium on Circuits and Systems,* 253–256.

3 Zeiler, M.D. and Fergus, R. (2013). Visualizing and Understanding Convolutional Networks. arXiv:1311.2901v3.

4 Gao, H. (2017). A walk-through of AlexNet, 7 August 2017 [Online]. https://medium.com/@smallfishbigsea/a-walk-through-of-alexnet-6cbd137a5637.

5 邱錫鵬, "神經網絡與深度學習 (2019). Neural Networks and Deep Learning, github [Online]. https://nndl.github.io.

6 Alom, M.Z., Taha, T.M., Yakopcic, C., et al. (2018). The History Began from AlexNet: A Comprehensive Survey on Deep Learning Approaches. arXiv:803.01164v2.

7 Sze, V., Chen, Y.-H., Yang, Y.-H., and Emer, J.S. (2017). Efficient processing of deep neural networks: a tutorial and survey. *Proceedings of the IEEE* 105 (12): 2295–2329.

8 Abdelouahab, K., Pelcat, M., Serot, J., and Berry, F. (2018). Accelerating CNN Inference on FPGA: A Survey. arXiv:1806.01683v1.

3

Parallel Architecture

This chapter describes several popular parallel architectures, Intel CPU, NVIDIA GPU, Google TPU, and Microsoft NPU. Intel CPU is designed for general computation and NVIDIA GPU is targeted for graphical display. However, they both employ a new memory structure with software support for deep learning applications. Custom design, Google TPU, and Microsoft NPU apply novel architectures to resolve deep learning computational challenges.

3.1 Intel Central Processing Unit (CPU)

Traditionally, the central processing unit (CPU) is targeted for general-purpose computation. It is evolved from Single Instruction Single Data (SISD) architecture to Single Instruction Multiple Data (SIMD) one to support parallel processing in recent years. However, it can't fulfill the deep learning massively parallel requirement through the multiple core and multiple thread approaches. In 2017, Intel developed a new Xeon processor scalable family [1–3] (Purley platform) to support deep learning applications (Table 3.1):

- Support 28 physical cores per socket (56 threads) at 2.5 GHz and up to 3.8 GHz at turbo mode
- Six memory channels support up to 1.5 Tb 2.666 GHz DDR4 memory
- 1 Mb private cache (L2 cache) and 38.5 Mb shared cache (L3 or Last-Level Cache – LLC)
- Operate at 3.57 TFLOPS (FP32) up to 5.18 TOPS (INT8) per socket and max 41.44 TOPS (INT8)
- Vector engine supports 512 bits wide Fused Multiply–Add (FMA) instructions

Artificial Intelligence Hardware Design: Challenges and Solutions, First Edition.
Albert Chun Chen Liu and Oscar Ming Kin Law.
© 2021 The Institute of Electrical and Electronics Engineers, Inc. Published 2021
by John Wiley & Sons, Inc.

Table 3.1 Intel Xeon family comparison.

Features	Intel Xeon processor ES2600 product Family	Intel Xeon processor scalable family
Platform	Grantley	Purley
CPU TDP	55–145 W, 160 W WS only	45–205 W
Socket	Socket R3	Socket P
Scalability	2S	2S, 4S, 8S
Cores	Up to 22 cores with Intel HT Technology	Up to 28 cores with Intel HT Technology
Mid-level cache	256 kb private cache	1 mb private cache
Last-level cache	Up to 2.5 mb/core (inclusive)	Up to 1.375 mb/core (non-inclusive)
Memory	4 channels DDR4 per CPU RDIMM, LRDIMM 1 DPC = 2400, 2 DPC = 2400, 3 DPC = 1866	6 channels DDR4 per CPU RDIMM, LRDIMM 2 DPC = 2133, 2400, 2666, No 3 DPC support
Point-to-point link	Intel QPI: 2 channels/CPU, 9.6 GT/s max	Intel UPI: 2–3 channels/CPU, 9.6–10.4 GT/s max
PCIe	PCIe 3.0 (2.5, 5.0, 8.0 GT/s) 40 lanes/CPU	PCIe 3.0 (2.5, 5.0, 8.0 GT/s) 48 lanes per CPU, Bifunction support: ×16, ×8, ×4
PCH	Wellsburg DM12–4 lanes, 6 × USB3, 8 × USB2 10 × SATA3, GbE MAC (External PHY)	Lewisburg DM13–4 lanes, 14 × USB2, 10 × USB3 14 × SATA3, 20 × PCIe3, 20 × 10 GbE
External controller	None	3rd party node controller

The major deep learning enhancements:

- Skylake mesh architecture
- Intel Ultra Path Interconnect (Intel UPI)
- SubNon-Unified Memory Access Clustering (SNC)
- Cache hierarchy changes
- Lower precision arithmetic operation
- Advanced vector software extension[1]
- Math Kernel Library for Deep Neural Network (MKL-DNN)

---

1 New Vector Neural Network Instruction (VNNI) in 2nd-generation Intel Xeon scalable family.

New Xeon processor broke the record that trained the ResNet-50 model in 31 minutes and AlexNet model in 11 minutes. Compared with the previous-generation Xeon processor, it improves training 2.2× and inference 2.4× throughput with the ResNet-18 model using the Intel Neon™ framework.

3.1.1 Skylake Mesh Architecture

In the previous generation, Intel Xeon processor (Grantley platform) connects CPU cores, Last-Level Cache (LLC), memory controller, I/O controller, and other peripherals using Intel Quick Path Interconnect (QPI) ring architecture (Figure 3.1). As the number of cores increases, the memory latency is increased with the available bandwidth per core diminished. The second ring is introduced to partition the processor into two halves for performance improvement. However, the single-core communication occupies the whole path resulting in high latency. Intel Scalable Xeon processor (Purley platform) upgrades to Intel Ultra Path Interconnect (UPI) mesh architecture to resolve the latency and bandwidth issues. Caching and Home Agent are integrated together to form a new Combined Home Agent (CHA) to resolve the memory bottleneck. CHA maps the address to the corresponding LLC banks, memory controller, and I/O controller. It provides the routing information for a destination using mesh interconnect (Figure 3.2).

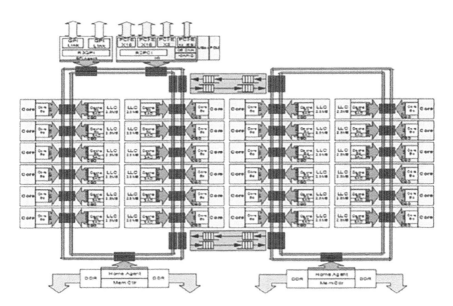

Figure 3.1 Intel Xeon processor ES 2600 family Grantley platform ring architecture [3].

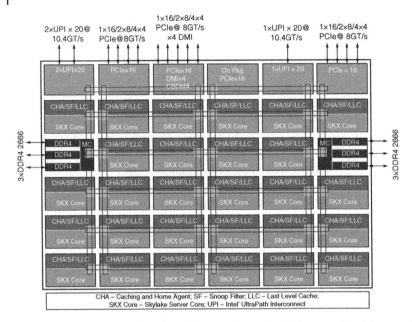

Figure 3.2 Intel Xeon processor scalable family Purley platform mesh architecture [3].

3.1.2 Intel Ultra Path Interconnect (UPI)

New Intel UPI is a multiple processor coherent interconnect with sharing address. It allows the data to transverse from one core to another through the shortest route using either vertical or horizontal paths. It can connect the processors in many ways: two-socket configuration, four-socket ring configuration, four-socket crossbar configuration, and eight-socket configuration. It provides the multiple data transfer at 10.4 GT/s using new packetization (Figures 3.3–3.6).

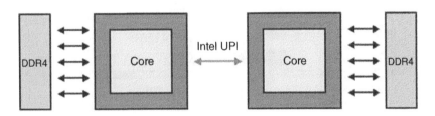

Figure 3.3 Two-socket configuration.

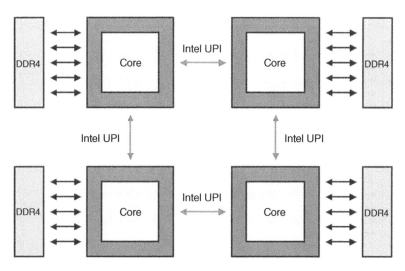

Figure 3.4 Four-socket ring configuration.

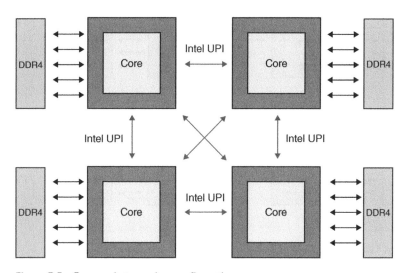

Figure 3.5 Four-socket crossbar configuration.

3.1.3 Sub Non-unified Memory Access Clustering (SNC)

Sub Non-Unified Memory Access Clustering (SNC) connects two localization domains together. SNC has a unique LLC address that maps to the memory controllers in the same socket. Compared with its predecessor, it significantly reduces memory and Last Level Cache (LLC) latency for remote access. All the remote

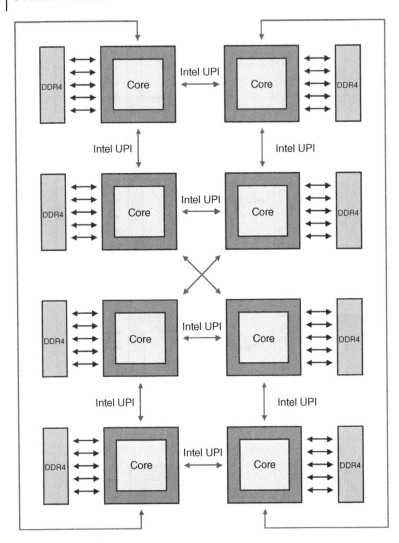

Figure 3.6 Eight-socket configuration.

socket addresses are uniformly distributed across LLC banks independent of SNC mode. The overall efficiency is improved through large LLC storage.

Two-domain configuration consists of SNC domains 0 and 1. Each supports half of the processor cores, half of LLC banks, and one memory controller with three DDR4 channels. It allows the system to effectively schedule the tasks and allocate the memory for optimal performance (Figure 3.7).

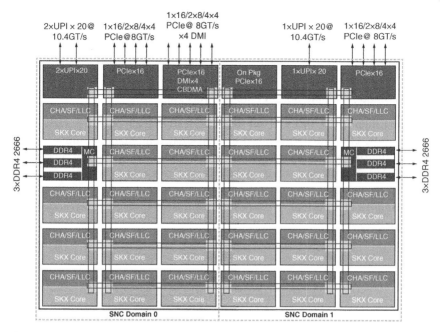

Figure 3.7 Sub-NUMA cluster domains [3].

3.1.4 Cache Hierarchy Changes

For the new Intel scalable Xeon processor, it provides 1 Mb private Mid-Level Cache (MLC) and 1.375 Mb LLC (Figure 3.8). It significantly improves the hit rate to reduce memory latency as well as mesh interconnect demands. It allows better cache utilization compared to inclusive shared LCC. For a miss, the data is fetched from memory into the MLC, the data is placed into LLC if it is expected to reuse.

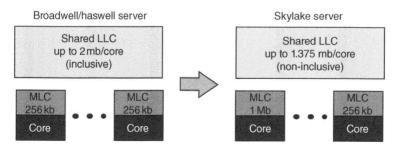

Figure 3.8 Cache hierarchy comparison.

Unlike its predecessor, the data is copied to both MLC and LLC banks. Due to the non-inclusive LLC nature, a snoop filter keeps track of cache line information for the absence of a cache line in the LLC bank.

3.1.5 Single/Multiple Socket Parallel Processing

With the high-speed UPI and sub-NUMA clustering support, the socket and cores can be efficiently partitioned to individual computational units [4] and run multiple deep learning training/inference (call worker processes) in parallel (Figure 3.9). The worker processes are assigned to a set of the cores and local memory on a single socket or multiple one. The overall performance is significantly improved with four workers/node compared to one worker/node baseline (Figure 3.10).

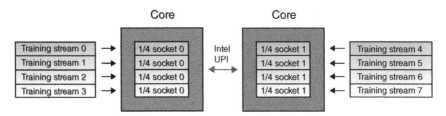

Figure 3.9 Intel multiple sockets parallel processing.

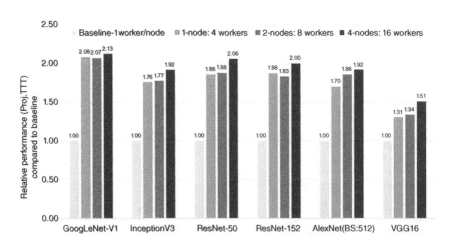

Figure 3.10 Intel multiple socket training performance comparison [4].

3.1.6 Advanced Vector Software Extension

Intel Advanced Vector Extension 512 (Intel AVX-512) supports two floating-point FMA units. These instructions allow the lower precision number (eight bits and 16 bits) to multiply together and convert into a higher precision one (32 bits). For example, both eight bits (VPMADDUBSW + VPMADDWD + VPADDD) and 16 bits (VPMADDWD + VPADDD) perform FMA operation within three and two clock cycle. Intel develops new AVX-512_VNNI Vector Neural Network Instruction [5] to simplify FMA operations, both eight bits (VDDPBUSD) and 16 bits (VPDPWSSD) instructions can perform multiply and add operations within a single cycle (Figures 3.11 and 3.12).

Intel new AVX-512 instructions further expand the operation from 256 –512 bits. AVX512DQ instructions enhance double/quad word integer and floating-point vectorization (i.e. sixteen 32 bits or eight 64 bits elements). It eliminates additional load/store operations for runtime reduction. AVX512BW instructions support the byte/word arithmetic operations and masking. AVX-512 instructions, also known as Vector Length Extensions, operate on 128 bits or 256 bits rather than 512 bits only. It fully utilizes XMM (128-bit SSE) register and YMM (256-bit AVX) operations.

Intel Advanced Vector Extension 512 features are listed as follows:

- Two 512 bits FMA instruction
- VNNI supports

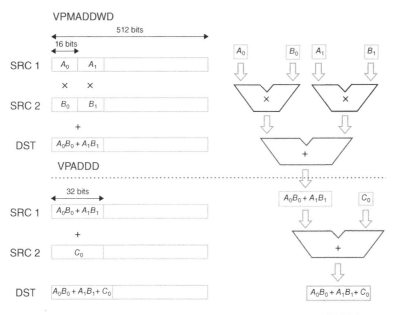

Figure 3.11 Intel AVX-512 16 bits FMA operations (VPMADDWD + VPADDD).

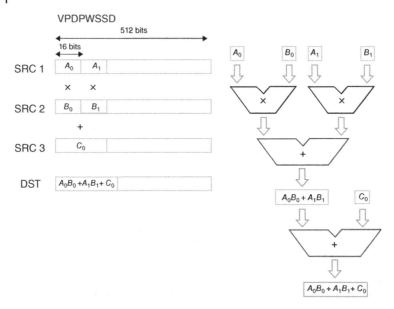

Figure 3.12 Intel AVX-512 with VNNI 16 bits FMA operation (VPDPWSSD).

- 512 bits floating-point and integer operations
- 32 registers
- 8 mask registers
- 64 bits single-precision and 32 bits double-precision FLOPS/cycle (with two 512 bits FMA)
- 32 bits single-precision and 16 bits double-precision FLOPS/cycle (with one 512 bits FMA)
- Embedded rounding
- Embedded broadcast
- Scale/SSE/AVX "promotions"
- Native media byte/word additions (AVX512BW)
- High-performance computing double/quadword additions (AVX512DQ)
- Mathematic transcendental support (i.e. π)
- Gather/Scatter

3.1.7 Math Kernel Library for Deep Neural Network (MKL-DNN)

Intel Math Kernel Library for Deep Neural Network (MKL-DNN) is optimized for deep learning basic functions (known as primitives). It consists of inner product, convolution, pooling (maximum, minimum, average), activation (Softmax, Rectified Linear Unit – ReLU), and batch normalization. The key features are

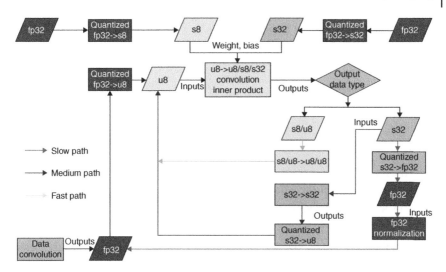

Figure 3.13   Intel low-precision convolution.

prefetching, data reuse, cache blocking, data layout, vectorization, and register blocking. Prefetching and data reuse avoid the same data multiple fetching to reduce the memory access. Cache blocking fits the data block into the cache to maximize the computation. Data layout arranges data consecutively in memory to avoid unnecessary data gather/scatter during the looping operation. It provides better cache utilization and improves prefetching operation. The vectorization restricts the outer looping dimension to be a multiple of SIMD width and inner looping over groups of SIMD width for effective computation. With optimal MKL-DNN library, the overall training and inference using Intel Xeon scalable processor (Intel Xeon Platinum 8180 Processor) significantly outperform its predecessor (Intel Xeon Processor ES-2699 v4) (Figure 3.13).

Recently, the Intel MKL-DNN library has been updated for inference with lower numerical precision [6]. It implements eight bits convolution with unsigned eight bits (u8) activation with signed eight bits (s8) weights to speed up the overall operations. For training, it still supports 32 bits floating-point convolution to achieve better accuracy. This approach optimizes the numerical precision for both training and inference.

The quantization transforms the non-negative activation and weight from 32 bits floating point to signed eight bits integer. It first calculates the quantization factors:

$$R_x = \max\left(abs\left(x\right)\right) \tag{3.1}$$

$$R_w = \max\left(abs\left(w\right)\right) \tag{3.2}$$

$$Q_x = \frac{255}{R_x} \tag{3.3}$$

$$Q_w = \frac{255}{R_w} \tag{3.4}$$

where

R_x is the maximum of the activation x
R_w is the maximum of the weights w
Q_x is the quantization factor of the activation x
Q_w is the quantization factor of the weights w

Then, the quantified activation x, weights w, and bias b is rounded to the nearest integer

$$a \cdot x_{u8} = \left\| Q_x x_{fp32} \right\| \quad \in \left[0, 255\right] \tag{3.5}$$

$$w_{s8} = \left\| Q_w w_{fp32} \right\| \quad \in \left[-128, 127\right] \tag{3.6}$$

$$b_{s32} = \left\| Q_x Q_w b_{fp32} \right\| \quad \in \left[-2^{31}, 2^{31} - 1\right] \tag{3.7}$$

where

x_{u8} is the unsigned eight bits integer activation
x_{fp32} is the 32 bits floating-point activation
w_{s8} is the signed eight bits integer weights
w_{fp32} is the 32 bits floating-point weights
b_{s32} is the signed 32 bits integer bias
‖ ‖ is the rounding operation

The integer computation is done using eight bits multiplier and 32 bits accumulator with the rounding approximation

$$y_{s32} = w_{s8} x_{u8} + b_{s32} \tag{3.8}$$

$$y_{s32} \approx Q_x Q_w \left(w_{fp32} x_{fp32} + b_{fp32}\right) \tag{3.9}$$

$$y_{s32} \approx Q_x Q_w y_{sp32} \tag{3.10}$$

Where

y_{s32} is the 32 bits signed integer output
x_{fp32} is the 32 bits floating-point activation

w_{fp32} is the 32 bits floating-point weights
b_{fp32} is the 32 bits floating-point bias

This approach significantly simplifies the hardware design with a similar accuracy range. The floating-point output can be obtained using the dequantization factor D

$$y_{\text{fp32}} = w_{fp32} x_{fp32} + b_{\text{fp32}} \tag{3.11}$$

$$y_{fp32} = \frac{1}{Q_x Q_w} y_{s32} \tag{3.12}$$

$$y_{fp32} = D y_{s32} \tag{3.13}$$

$$D = \frac{1}{Q_x Q_w} \tag{3.14}$$

where

y_{fp32} is 32 bits floating-point output
D is the dequantization factor

It is modified to support the activation with a negative value

$$R_{x'} = \max\left(abs\left(x'\right)\right) \tag{3.15}$$

$$Q_{x'} = \frac{255}{R_{x'}} \tag{3.16}$$

Where

x' is the activation with a negative value
$R_{x'}$ is the maximum of the activation
$Q_{x'}$ is the quantization factor of the activation

The activation and weights are changed

$$x_{s8} = Q_{x'} x_{fp32} \quad \in \left[-128, 127\right] \tag{3.17}$$

$$x_{u8} = \text{shift}\left(x_{s8}\right) \quad \in \left[0, 255\right] \tag{3.18}$$

$$b'_{fp32} = b_{fp32} - \frac{\text{shift}\left(W_{fp32}\right)}{Q_{x'}} \tag{3.19}$$

$$w_{s8} = Q_w w_{fp32} \quad \in \left[-128, 127\right] \tag{3.20}$$

$$b'_{s32} = Q_{x'} Q_w b'_{fp32} \quad \in \left[-2^{31}, 2^{31} - 1\right] \tag{3.21}$$

where

b'_{s32} is the 32 bits signed integer supported the negative activation

b'_{fp32} is the 32 bits floating-point bias supporting the negative activation shift which performs the shift left operation to scale up the number

With the same eight bits multipliers and 32 bits accumulators, the calculation is defined as

$$y_{s32} = w_{s8}x_{u8} + b'_{s32} \tag{3.22}$$

$$y_{s32} \approx Q_{x'}Q_w\left(w_{fp32}x_{fp32} + b_{fp32}\right) \tag{3.23}$$

$$y_{s32} \approx Q_{x'}Q_w y_{sp32} \tag{3.24}$$

and the floating-point output is calculated with a similar dequantization process

$$y_{fp32} = w_{fp32}x_{fp32} + b_{fp32} \tag{3.11}$$

$$y_{fp32} = \frac{1}{Q_{x'}Q_w} y_{s32} \tag{3.12}$$

$$yfp_{32} = Dys_{32} \tag{3.13}$$

$$D = \frac{1}{Q_{x'}Q_w} \tag{3.14}$$

With the lower numerical precision Intel MKL-DNN library, both training and inference throughput are twice as the predecessor. The software optimization dramatically improves the overall system performance with less power (Figures 3.14 and 3.15).

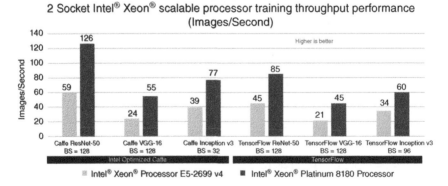

Figure 3.14 Intel Xenon processor training throughput comparison [2].

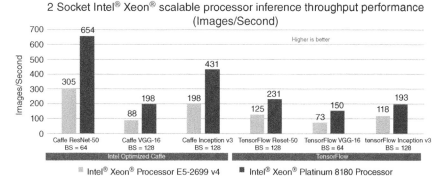

Figure 3.15 Intel Xenon processor inference throughput comparison [2].

3.2 NVIDIA Graphics Processing Unit (GPU)

NVIDIA Graphics Processing Unit (GPU) is widely applied for deep learning applications (i.e. image classification, speech recognition, and self-driving vehicle) due to effective floating-point computation and high-speed memory support (Figure 3.16). With new Turing architecture [7], it speeds up the deep learning training and inference arithmetic operation to 14.2 TFLOPS (FP32) and supports high-speed NVLink2 for HBM2 (2nd-generation High Bandwidth Memory) with 900 Gb/s bandwidth. Turing Multi-Process Service further improves overall performance through a hardware accelerator. New neural graphics framework NVIDIA NGX™ with NGX DLSS (Deep Learning Super-Sample) accelerates and enhances the graphics, rendering, and other applications (Table 3.2).

The key features of Turing architecture based on TU102 GPU (GeForce RTX-2080) are listed as follows:

- Six Graphics Processing Clusters (GPC)
- Each GPC has Texture Processing Clusters (TPC) with two Streaming Multiprocessors (SM) per TPC
- Total 34 TPC and 68 SM
- Each SM has 64 CUDA Cores, eight Tensor Cores, and an additional 68 Ray Tracing (RT) Cores
- GPU clock speed: 1350 MHz
- 14.2 TFLOPS of single-precision (FP32) performance
- 28.5 TFLOPS of half-precision (FP16) performance
- 14.2 TIPS concurrent with FP, through independent integer execution units
- 113.8 Tensor TFLOPS

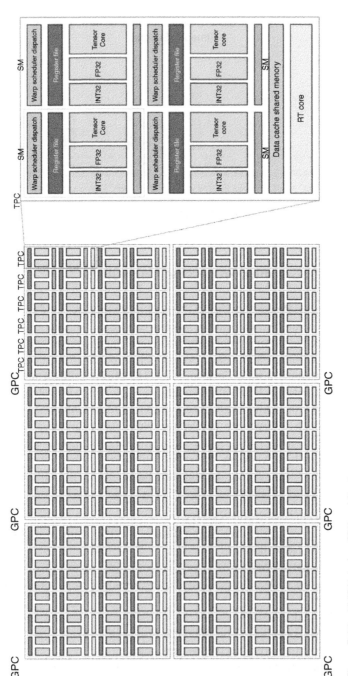

Figure 3.16 NVIDIA turing GPU architecture.

Table 3.2 NVIDIA GPU architecture comparison.

GPU	Tesla P100	Tesla V100	Tesla TU102
Architecture	Pascal	Volta	Turing
GPCs	6	6	6
TPCs	28	40	34
SMs	56	80	68
CUDA cores/SM	128	128	64
CUDA cores/GPU	3584	5120	4352
Tensor cores/SM	NA	8	8
Tensor cores/GPU	NA	640	544
RT Cores	NA	NA	68
Clock (MHz)	1480	1530	1350

With the additional integer data-path, Turing architecture supports concurrent INT32 and FP32 mixed-precision arithmetic operations and avoids floating-point instruction blocking issue. New unified share memory architecture is introduced, the larger 64 kb shared memory not only increases the memory hit rate but also leverages out resource. The L1 cache is reconfigured with a larger capacity when the shared memory is not fully utilized. Equivalently, it increases 2× memory bandwidth as well as 2× L1 cache capacity. The architecture is significantly enhanced from Pascal [8], Volta [9] to Turing GPU (Figure 3.17).

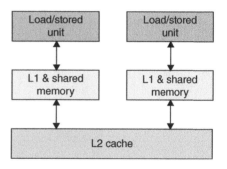

Figure 3.17 NVIDIA GPU shared memory.

3.2.1 Tensor Core Architecture

Unlike the Pascal core simultaneous multithreading (SMT) (GTX 1080), it multiplies the matrix row by row. Tensor Core performs $4 \times 4 \times 4$ matrix Multiply–Accumulate (MAC) operation, it multiplies two matrices at the same time using the SMT approach. It performs FP16 multiplication with FP32 product, then accumulates using FP32 addition as well as the partial sum. It speeds up the overall performance: FP16 (8×), INT8 (16×), and INT4 (32×) (Figures 3.18 and 3.19).

$$D = A \times B + C$$

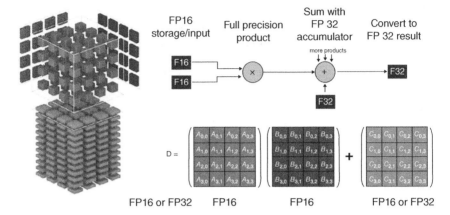

Figure 3.18 Tensor core 4 × 4 × 4 matrix operation [9].

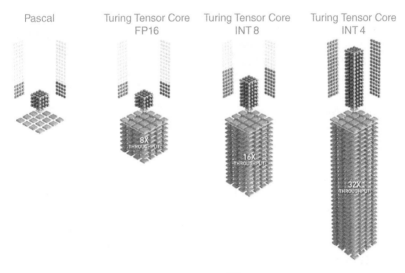

Figure 3.19 Turing tensor core performance [7].

For 16 × 16 matrix multiplication [10], it first divides the matrix into eight thread groups of four threads. Each group computes 8 × 4 blocks through four sets of operations. Through eight group computations, it creates 16 × 16 matrix (Figure 3.20).

Matrices A and B are first divided into multiple sets, then executes the instruction in Set 0, followed by Set 1, Set 2, and Set 3. Finally, it correctly computes 4 × 8 elements in Matrix D (Figure 3.21).

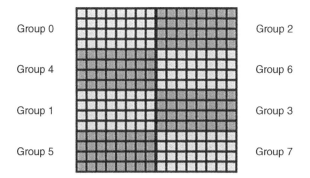

Group 0	Group 2
Group 4	Group 6
Group 1	Group 3
Group 5	Group 7

Figure 3.20 Matrix D thread group indices.

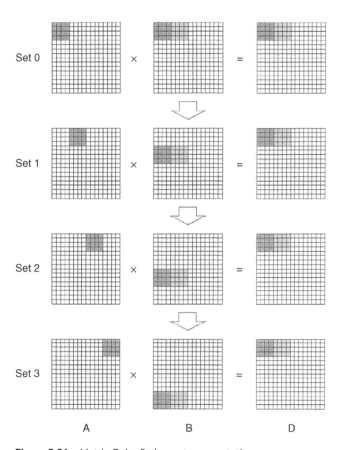

Set 0   ×   =

Set 1   ×   =

Set 2   ×   =

Set 3   ×   =

A   B   D

Figure 3.21 Matrix D 4 × 8 elements computation.

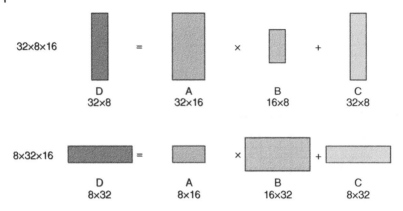

Figure 3.22 Different size matrix multiplication.

In addition to $16 \times 16 \times 16$ mixed-precision Matrix Multiply–Accumulation (MMA), Turing architecture offers an additional $32 \times 8 \times 16$ and $8 \times 32 \times 16$ configuration which makes it more feasible for different size matrix computation (Figure 3.22).

3.2.2 Winograd Transform

In order to minimize the convolution computation, Winograd transform [11, 12] is employed. It is derived from the m-outputs with r-tap 1D Finite Impulse Response (FIR) filter algorithm. For F(m,r) filter, $m + r - 1$ multiplications are required to compute the output. For Winograd 1D transform, F(2, 2) and F(2, 3) are defined as:

$$F(2,2) = \begin{bmatrix} d_0 & d_1 \\ d_1 & d_2 \end{bmatrix} \begin{bmatrix} g_0 \\ g_1 \end{bmatrix} \tag{3.15}$$

$$F(2,2) = \begin{bmatrix} m_1 + m_2 \\ m_2 - m_3 \end{bmatrix} \tag{3.16}$$

$$m_1 = (d_0 - d_1)g_0 \tag{3.17}$$

$$m_2 = d_1(g_0 + g_1) \tag{3.18}$$

$$m_3 = (d_1 - d_2)g_1 \tag{3.19}$$

The standard algorithm requires four multiplications and two additions but Winograd transform requires three multiplications and five additions

$$F(2,3) = \begin{bmatrix} d_0 & d_1 & d_2 \\ d_1 & d_2 & d_3 \end{bmatrix} \begin{bmatrix} g_0 \\ g_1 \\ g_2 \end{bmatrix} \tag{3.20}$$

$$F(2,3) = \begin{bmatrix} m_1 + m_2 + m_3 \\ m_2 - m_3 - m_4 \end{bmatrix} \tag{3.21}$$

$$m_1 = (d_0 - d_2)g_0 \tag{3.22}$$

$$m_2 = (d_1 + d_2)\frac{g_0 + g_1 + g_2}{2} \tag{3.23}$$

$$m_3 = (d_2 - d_1)\frac{g_0 - g_1 + g_2}{2} \tag{3.24}$$

$$m_4 = (d_1 - d_3)g_2 \tag{3.25}$$

The standard algorithm requires six multiplications and four additions and Winograd transform only requires four multiplications, 12 additions, and two shift operations. F(2, 3) is preferred over F(2, 2) for convolution computation due to its efficiency.

Winograd 1D algorithm is nested to support Winograd 2D convolution F(m × m, r × r) with r × r filter and the m × m input activation. It is partitioned into (m + r − 1) × (m + r − 1) tiles with r − 1 elements overlap between the neighboring tiles. The standard algorithm uses m × m × r × r multiplications but Winograd 2D convolution only requires (m + r − 1) × (m + r − 1) multiplications.

For F(2 × 2, 3 × 3) operations, the standard algorithm performs 2 × 2 × 3 × 3 multiplications (total 36) but Winograd 2D convolution only requires (2 + 3 − 1) × (2 + 3 − 1) multiplications (total 16). It is optimized for convolution and reduces the number of multiplications by 36/15 = 2.25 using 3 × 3 filter. However, the drawback of Winograd 2D convolutions requires different computations for various filter sizes.

3.2.3 Simultaneous Multithreading (SMT)

For SMT, the matrix is divided into multiple groups. It performs the matrix multiplication with a patch pattern for all subsets (fragments) (Figure 3.23). It launches the independent threads (also known as warp) in Single Instruction Multiple Thread (SIMT) fashion to compute the matrix subset in parallel and each subset

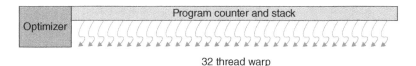

Optimizer | Program counter and stack

32 thread warp

Figure 3.23 Simultaneous multithreading (SMT).

does not interact with others. After the matrix multiplication, it regroups the subsets into the same group to obtain the results (Figure 3.24).

New SMT also supports the independent thread scheduling with scheduler optimizer in its own program counter and stack information. It determines how to group the active threads with the same warp to fully utilize the SIMT unit. For example, a new synchronization feature called syncwarp allows the thread to diverge and reconverge at a fine granularity to maximize parallel efficiency.

3.2.4 High Bandwidth Memory (HBM2)

Turing architecture employs HBM2 to resolve memory bottleneck. Unlike the discrete memory chip, HBM2 stacks multiple dies together using Through Silicon Via (TSV) to reduce the output load. The HBM2 is connected to GPU through NVLink2 (Figure 3.25).

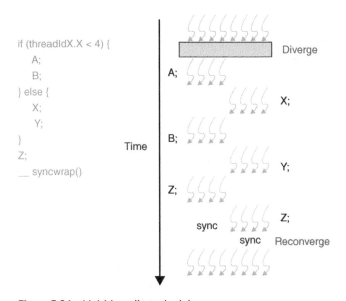

Figure 3.24 Multithreading schedule.

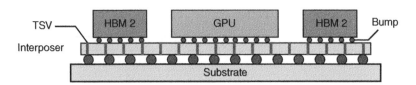

Figure 3.25 GPU with HBM2 architecture.

Compared to HBM1, HBM2 supports up to eight DRAM dies per stack. The memory size is increased from 2–8 Gb per die. The memory bandwidth is also increased from 125–180 Gb/s. The high-memory bandwidth dramatically enhances the overall GPU performance.

3.2.5 NVLink2 Configuration

Turing architecture replaces a single Multiple Input/Output (MIO) interface with two × 8 bidirectional differential pair NVLink2 for data transfer. It allows the direct load/store/atomic between CPU and GPU memory. The data directly reads from GPU memory and stores in the CPU cache. It improves CPU performance due to low latency access. NVLink2 supports GPU atomic operations that different threads manipulate the shared data for workload sharing. Each link provides 40 Gb/s peak bandwidth between two GPUs. NVLink2 is arranged in two different ways: GPU-to-GPU and GPU-to-CPU configurations. For GPU-to-GPU configuration, eight GPUs are arranged in hybrid cube mesh, two NVLink2 connects four GPUs together and each GPU connects to CPU through PCIe bus. It is operated as a share memory multiprocessor and the PCIe bus is available for system memory access. Similarly, four GPUs connect through NVLink mesh to achieve high throughput. For GPU-to-CPU configurations, a single GPU connects to the CPU through NVLink with 160 Gb/s bidirectional bandwidth. Two GPUs connect with the CPU and estimate peer-to-peer communication between two GPUs (Figures 3.26–3.29).

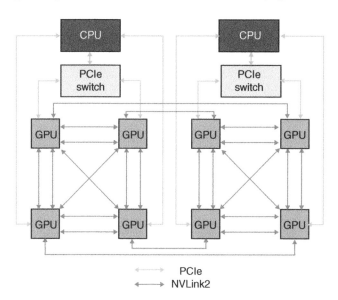

Figure 3.26 Eight GPUs NVLink2 configuration.

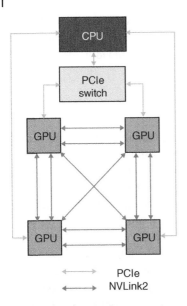

Figure 3.27 Four GPUs NVLink2 configuration.

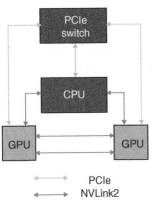

Figure 3.28 Two GPUs NVLink2 configuration.

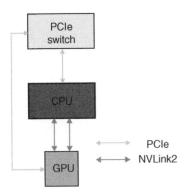

Figure 3.29 Single GPU NVLink2 configuration.

The NVLink2 successfully links CPUs and GPUs together to construct DGX-1 supercomputer. For example, NVIDIA DGX-1 with 8 GPUs (Tesla V100) and 2 CPUs (Intel Xeon E5-2698 v4 2.2 GHz) achieves over 1 PFLOPS performance for deep learning applications.

3.3 NVIDIA Deep Learning Accelerator (NVDLA)

NVIDIA Deep Learning Accelerator (NVDLA)[2] [13, 14] is an open-source configurable processor[3] for inference operations. It supports the Convolutional Neural Network (CNN) with four primitive functional blocks, convolution, activation, pooling, and normalization. Every block employs double buffers for active and next layer configuration. The next layer starts the new operation when the active operation is completed. All the blocks are configured in two modes, the independent mode and the fused mode. For independent mode, each block works independently with its own memory access. Fused mode operation is similar to an independent one. It is arranged in pipeline configuration to improve the overall performance (Figure 3.30).

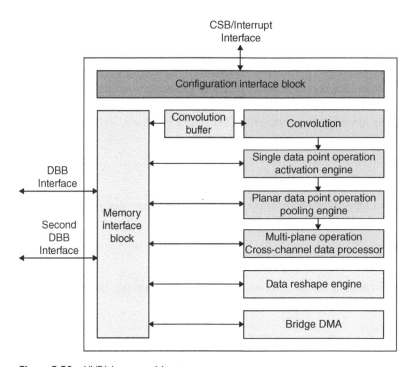

Figure 3.30 NVDLA core architecture.

---

2 http://nvdla.org
3 NVDLA accelerator is an open-source project which can be implemented using FPGA approach.

3.3.1 Convolution Operation

Convolution core works on the input feature data and trained weights. It supports four different convolutions:

- Direct convolution: Apply the wide MAC unit for direct convolution with space compression and on-chip second memory interface
- Image input convolution: Focus on three channel image inputs
- Winograd convolution: Support Winograd 2D transform to reduce the number of multiplications in convolution. The reduction factor is 2.25× for 3 × 3 convolution
- Batch convolution: Process multiple sets of inputs with a weight reuse approach to reduce the memory access

3.3.2 Single Data Point Operation

Single Data Point (SDP) supports the activation and the normalization through the linear functions (simple bias and scaling) as well as the Look-up Table (LUT) nonlinear functions:

- Linear function: Supports the precision scaling, batch normalization, bias addition, and elementwise operation. The precision scaling converts the number into lower precision computation to speed up the operation and the elementwise operation supports the basic operations (addition, subtraction, multiplication, and max/min comparison)
- Nonlinear function: Implements the activation functions, ReLU, PReLU, sigmoid, and hyperbolic tangent

3.3.3 Planar Data Operation

Planar Data Operation (PDP) supports different pooling operations and maximum/minimum/average pooling functions.

3.3.4 Multiplane Operation

The Cross-Channel Data Processor (CDP) performs the Local Response Normalization (LRN)

$$
\text{Result}_{w,h,c} = \frac{\text{Source}_{w,h,c}}{\left(j + \dfrac{\alpha}{n} \sum_{i=\max(0,c-\frac{n}{2})}^{\min(C-1,c+\frac{n}{2})} \text{Source}_{w,h,i}^2\right)^\beta}
\tag{3.26}
$$

3.3.5 Data Memory and Reshape Operations

The bridge DMA transfers the data between the external memory and memory interface. The data reshape engine performs the data transformations, splitting, slicing, merging, contraction, and reshape-transpose.

3.3.6 System Configuration

NVDLA accelerator can be configured in two system models. The small system model targets for IoT application. It strips down the neural network model to reduce the complexity with less storage and loading time but only performs the single task at a time (Figures 3.31 and 3.32).

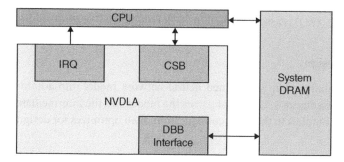

Figure 3.31 NVDLA small system model.

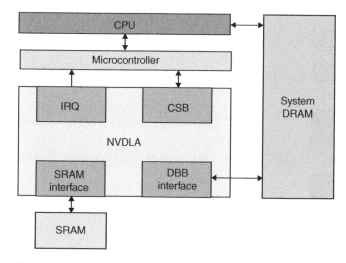

Figure 3.32 NVDLA large system model.

The large system model employs an additional coprocessor with the memory interface to support multiple task local operations. The memory interface connects to the high-bandwidth memory to reduce host loading.

3.3.7 External Interface

The NVDLA accelerator connects to the system through four interfaces:

- Configuration Space Bus (CSB) is a 32 bits low bandwidth control bus and allows the hosts to configure NDLA for operation
- Data Backbone (DDB) interface is a high-speed interface and allows NDLA accelerator to access the main memory
- SRAM Interface provides optional SRAM as the cache to improve the system performance
- Interrupt Interface (IRQ) is asserted when the task is completed or errors occur

3.3.8 Software Design

NVDLA software dataflow converts trained neural network model into a hardware implementation (Figure 3.33). It first parses the model into the intermediate representation and complies to the layer configuration, then optimizes for design

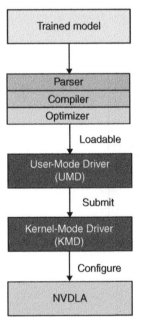

Figure 3.33 NVDLA software dataflow.

hardware. In order to run the models in NVDLA, it is divided into two modes, User Mode Driver (UMD) and Kernel Mode Driver (KMD). UMD loads the complied NVDLA loadable and submits the jobs to KMD. KMD schedules the layer operation and configures each functional block for inference operations.

3.4 Google Tensor Processing Unit (TPU)

Google successfully deployed Tensor Processing Unit (TPU) [15, 16] to resolve the growing demand for speech recognition in a datacenter in 2013. TPU is evolved from standalone v1 to cloud v2/v3 [17, 18] to support a wide range of deep learning applications today. The key features of TPU v1 are listed as below:

- 256×256 eight bits MAC unit
- 4 Mb on-chip Accumulator Memory (AM)
- 24 Mb Unified Buffer (UB) – activation memory
- 8 Gb off-chip weight DRAM memory
- Two 2133 MHz DDR3 channels

TPU v1 handles six different neural network applications that account for 95% of the workload:

- Multi-Layer Perceptron (MLP): The layer is a set of nonlinear weighted sum of prior layer outputs (fully connected) and reuses the weights
- Convolutional Neural Network (CNN): The layer is a set of nonlinear weighted sum of spatial nearby subsets of prior layer outputs and reuses the weights
- Recurrent Neural Network (RNN): The layer is a set of nonlinear weighted sum of prior layer outputs and previous set. The popular RNN is Long Short-Term Memory (LSTM) that determines what state can forget or pass to the next layer and reuses the weights (Table 3.3)

3.4.1 System Architecture

TPU v1 performs the matrix operations using Matrix Multiply Unit (MMU). It consists of 256×256 MAC unit for eight bits signed/unsigned integer multiply and add. It produces 256 partial sums per cycle and the 16 bits partial sums are stored in 32 bits 4 Mb accumulator. Due to the eight bits design, the performance is degraded by half for eight bits/16 bits mixed operation and becomes one-quarter for both 16 bits operation. However, TPU v1 does not support the sparse matrix multiplication (Figure 3.34).

The Weight FIFO reads the matrix weights from the off-chip 8 Gb DRAM (Weight Memory). After activation, pooling, and normalization, the intermediate results are stored in 24 Mb Unified Buffer and fed into MMU for the next computation (Figure 3.35).

Table 3.3 TPU v1 applications.

Name	Layers					Nonlinear function	Weights	Ops/Weight byte	Batch size	Deploy (%)
	Conv	Pool	FC	Vector	Total					
MLP0			5		5	ReLU	20 M	200	200	61
MLP1			4		4	ReLU	5 M	168	168	61
RNN0			24	34	58	Sigmoid, tanh	52 M	64	64	29
RNN1			37	29	66	Sigmoid, tanh	34 M	96	96	29
CNN0	16				16	ReLU	8 M	2888	8	5
CNN1	72	13	4		89	ReLU	100 M	1750	32	5

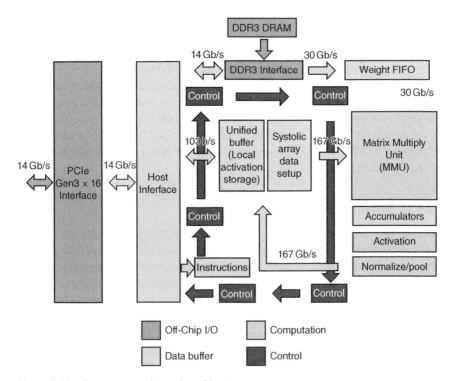

Figure 3.34 Tensor processing unit architecture.

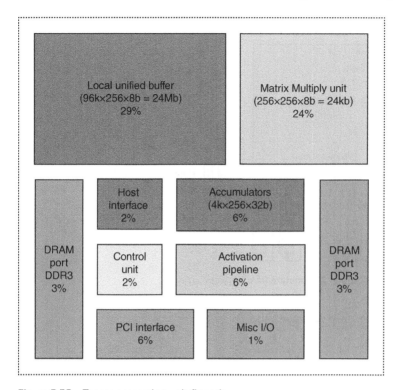

Figure 3.35   Tensor processing unit floorplan.

3.4.2   Multiply–Accumulate (MAC) Systolic Array

The heart of TPU v1 is the 256 × 256 MAC unit derived from the systolic array [19, 20]. It is an SIMD highly pipeline computational network with high through-put low latency. The systolic array is an analogy on how blood rhythmically flows through a biological heart as data transfers from memory to Processing Element (PE) in a rhythmic fashion. All the data is skewed and synchronized by a global clock and feeds into a systolic array for computation. The results are available in pipeline fashion and well suitable for matrix multiplication. The drawback of a systolic array is high-power dissipation because of simultaneous operations. TPU is a good choice for datacenter applications (Figures 3.36 and 3.37).

3.4.3   New Brain Floating-Point Format

Floating-point hardware requires additional exponent alignment, normalization, rounding, and long-carry propagation [21]. TPU v1 quantizes the input data from FP32 to INT8 with the advantage of speed, area, and power. The major drawback

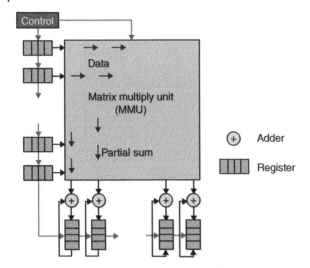

Figure 3.36 Multiply–Accumulate (MAC) systolic array.

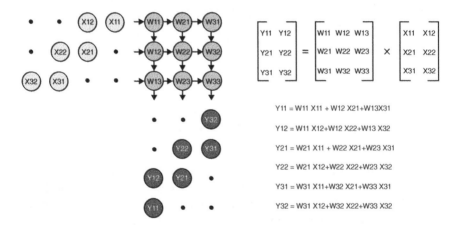

Figure 3.37 Systolic array matrix multiplication.

of quantization is the integer truncation error as well as numerical instability (Figure 3.38).

In order to resolve the numerical instability, Google replaces 16 bits half-precision IEEE Floating-Point Format (FP16) with 16 bits Brain Floating-Point Format (BFP16). The small mantissa significantly reduces multiplier area and power but achieves the same dynamic range as 32 bits Single-Precision Floating-Point Format (FP32). It also reduces memory storage and saves overall bandwidth. With BFP16, it keeps the same accuracy as FP32 without scaling loss (Figure 3.39).

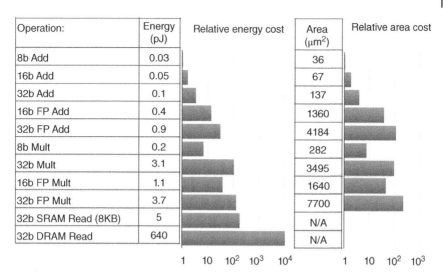

Operation:	Energy (pJ)	Relative energy cost	Area (μm^2)	Relative area cost
8b Add	0.03		36	
16b Add	0.05		67	
32b Add	0.1		137	
16b FP Add	0.4		1360	
32b FP Add	0.9		4184	
8b Mult	0.2		282	
32b Mult	3.1		3495	
16b FP Mult	1.1		1640	
32b FP Mult	3.7		7700	
32b SRAM Read (8KB)	5		N/A	
32b DRAM Read	640		N/A	

Figure 3.38 Cost of different numerical format operation.

IEEE 32 Bits Single Precision Floating Point Format : FP32   Range: ~1e-38 to ~3e38

Sign: 1 bit, Exponent: 8 bits, Mantissa: 23 bits

IEEE 16 Bits Half Precision Floating Point Format : FP16   Range: ~5.96e-8 to 65504

Sign: 1 bit, Exponent: 5 bits, Mantissa: 10 bits

Google 16 Bits Brain Floating Point Format : BFP16   Range: ~1e-38 to ~3e38

Sign: 1 bit, Exponent: 8 bits, Mantissa: 7 bits

Figure 3.39 TPU brain floating-point format.

3.4.4 Performance Comparison

To illustrate the performance comparison among CPU, GPU, and TPU, the roof-line model [22] is adopted. For roofline model, the Y-axis represents the floating-point operations where the peak performance is identified as the "flat" part of the roofline, the X-axis shows the operation intensity measured in floating-point operations per byte. This approach determines the peak performance limit.

From the roofline model, TPU achieves a higher peak performance than CPU (Intel Haswell) and GPU (NVIDIA K80) because both CPU and GPU are limited

Log-Log scale

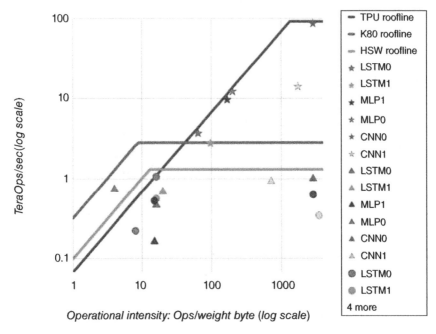

Figure 3.40 CPU, GPU, and TPU performance comparison [15].

by the memory bandwidth. TPU simplifies the hardware design without sophistical microarchitecture, memory translation, and multithreading supports (Figure 3.40).

3.4.5 Cloud TPU Configuration

Google extends standalone TPU v1 to cloud TPU v2 and v3 for datacenter applications. For cloud TPU v2 and v3, it replaces DDR3 memory with high bandwidth memory (HBM) to resolve the memory bottleneck. For TPU pod configuration, it connects multiple TPU cores through a dedicated high-speed network to improve the overall performance. The TPU cores are connected without the host CPU and network resource. For TPU v2 pod, the pod employs 128 TPU v2 cores. It is increased to 256 TPU v3 cores for TPU v3 pod with additional 32 Tb memory. The performance is significantly improved from the TPU v2 pod to the TPU v3 one (Figures 3.41–3.43; Table 3.4).

TPU v2 and v3 employ the new 128 × 128 Matrix Unit (MXU). It performs 16k multiply–accumulate operations per cycle. The 32 bits standard floating-point

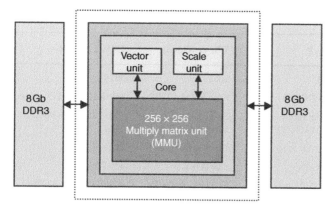

Figure 3.41 Tensor Processing Unit (TPU) v1.

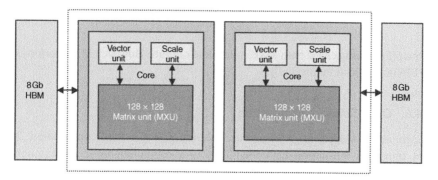

Figure 3.42 Tensor Processing Unit (TPU) v2.

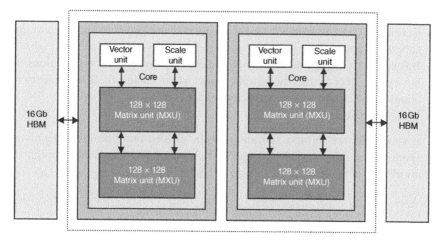

Figure 3.43 Tensor Processing Unit (TPU) v3.

Table 3.4 Tensor processing unit comparison.

Version	TPU v1	TPU v2 (Cloud)	TPU v3 (Cloud)
Design	2015	2017	2018
Core memory	8 Gb DRAM / TPU	8 Gb HBM / TPU	16 Gb HBM / TPU core
Processor element	Single 256 × 256 MAC / TPU	Single 128 × 128 MXU / TPU	Two 128 × 128 MXU / TPU
CPU interface	PCIe 3.0 × 16	PCIe 3.0 × 8	PCIe 3.0 × 8
Performance	92 TOPS	180 TOPS	420 TOPS
Pod cluster	N/A	512 TPU and 4 Tb memory	2048 TPU and 32 Tb memory
Application	Inference	Training and inference	Training and inference

format (FP32) is used for both MXU inputs and outputs. However, MXU performs BFP16 multiplication internally.

3.4.6 Cloud Software Architecture

Google also develops new software architecture [23] for cloud computation. It first translates the neural network model to a computational graph through TensorFlow. The TensorFlow server determines how many TPU cores are available for computation with the following steps:

- Load the inputs from the cloud storage
- Partition the graph into a different portion for Cloud TPU operation
- Generates XLA (Accelerated Linear Algebra) operations corresponding to the subgraph operator
- Invoke XLA compiler to convert High-Level Optimizer (HLO) operations to binary code. It optimizes the runtime types and dimension, fuses multiple operations together, and generates efficient native code.
- Run-on distributive Cloud TPUs

For example, the softmax activation can be divided into primitive operations (exponent, reduction, and elementwise division). XLA[4] can further optimize TensorFlow subgraph through fused operations. The subgraphs can be

4 Google applies software approach to optimize the TensorFlow subgraph. Blaize GSP and Graphcore IPU realize the similar approach through hardware design in Chapter 4.

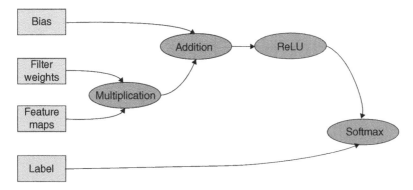

Figure 3.44 Google TensorFlow subgraph optimization.

implemented using an efficient loop with a minimal number of kernels without additional memory allocation. It speeds up the performance by 50% over the GPU approach (Figure 3.44).

3.5 Microsoft Catapult Fabric Accelerator

With the growth of speech search demand, Microsoft initializes the Brainwave project to develop low-cost and highly efficient datacenter with Azure Network using the Catapult fabric [24–26] accelerator for different applications (Figure 3.45):

- Local computation accelerator
- Network/storage accelerator
- Remote computational accelerator

Brainwave architecture targets for hyperscale datacenter which connects the CPU with custom FPGA. Multiple FPGAs are grouped as a shared microservice resource to handle scalable workloads. It provides a better load balance between CPU and FPGA. 48 FPGAs are organized in two half racks called pods and connected using a 6×8 tour network with 8 Gb DRAM support for local computation (Figure 3.46).

Brainwave first compiles the pretrained DNN model into the synthesized softcore called the Catapult fabric, then applies the narrow precision approach to speed up the operation. The model parameters are fully resided in the softcore to minimize memory access (Figure 3.47).

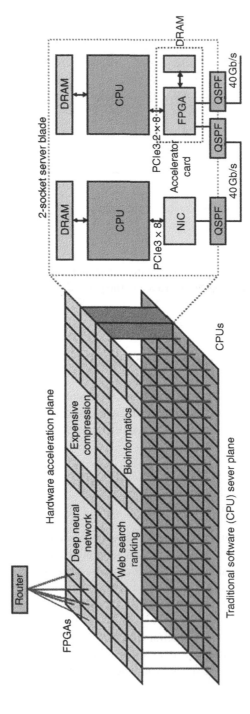

Figure 3.45 Microsoft Brainwave configurable cloud architecture.

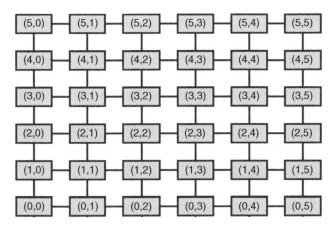

Figure 3.46 Tour network topology.

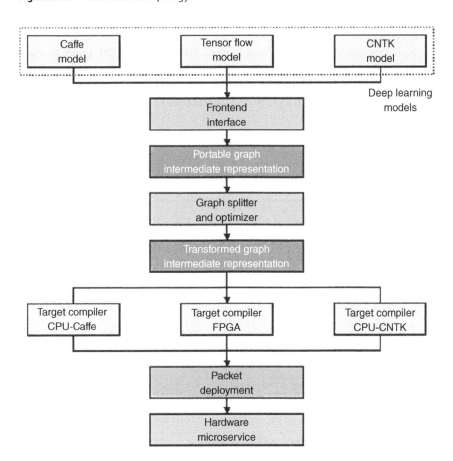

Figure 3.47 Microsoft Brainwave design flow.

3.5.1 System Configuration

The Catapult fabric is a synthesized softcore. It can be reconfigured using low-level software library to simplify the hardware design without RTL recompilation for the desired applications. The Catapult fabric is divided into two partitions: the shell and the role. The shell is a reusable programmable logic common across all applications. The role is the application logic to access the shell functions through the programming interface. The key features of the shell are highlighted as follows:

- Two DRAM controllers work independently or act as a unified interface
- Four high-speed serial links support SerialLite III (SL3) interface
- Lightweight Transport Layer (LTL) enables inter-FPGA communication between neighboring FPGA. It supports FIFO semantics, Xon/Xoff flow control and Error-Correcting Code Memory (ECC)
- Elastic Router (ER) with virtual channel allows multiple roles to access the network
- Reconfigurable logic derived from Remote Status Update (RSU) unit to read/write the configuration flash
- The PCIe core links with the CPU and supports the DMA
- Single-Event Upset (SEU) logic periodically scrubs FPGA configuration to avoid soft errors (Figure 3.48)

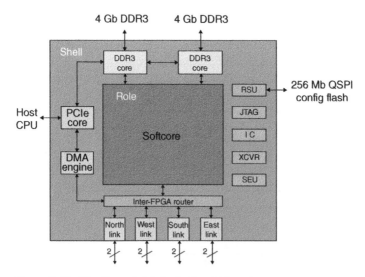

Figure 3.48 The Catapult fabric shell architecture.

3.5.2 Catapult Fabric Architecture

The Catapult fabric is derived from the single thread vector processor architecture with Matrix-Vector Multiplier (MVM), the multifunction unit (MFU), and vector arbitration networks. MVM can perform both matrix-vector and vector-vector multiplication. The Pipeline Register Files (PRFs), Vector Register Files (VRFs), and Matrix Register Files (MRFs) store the input feature maps and the filter weights (Figure 3.49).

Vector arbitration network manages the data transfer among PRFs, DRAM, and neighbor I/O queue. Top-level scheduler with input instruction chain controls the functional unit operation and the vector arbitration network.

3.5.3 Matrix-Vector Multiplier

The MVM is the key computational unit of the Catapult fabric (Figure 3.50). It employs dedicated memory to resolve the memory bandwidth and throughput

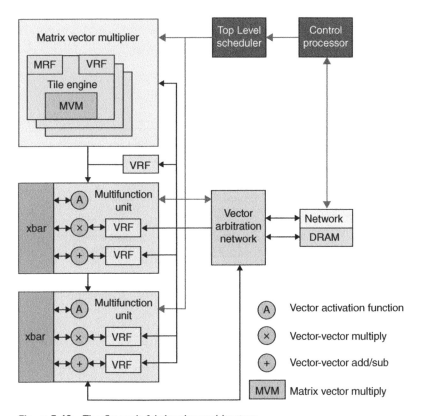

Figure 3.49 The Catapult fabric microarchitecture.

issues. It converts FP16 input data into Microsoft narrow precision format (MS-FP8/MS-FP9) like Google BF16 format. MS-FP8/MS-FP9 are referred to eight bits and nine bits floating-point format where the mantissa is truncated to two or three bits only. This format can achieve higher accuracy with a better dynamic range. It employs multiple tile engines to support native size matrix-vector multiplication. The input data is loaded into the VRFs and the filter weights are stored in the MRFs for multiplication (Figure 3.51).

Each tile engine is supported by a series of the Dot-Product Engine (DPE). It multiplies the input vector with one row in matrix tile. The results are fed to an

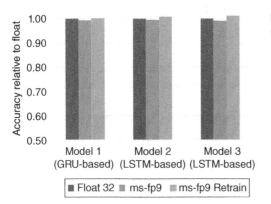

Figure 3.50 Microsoft low-precision quantization [27].

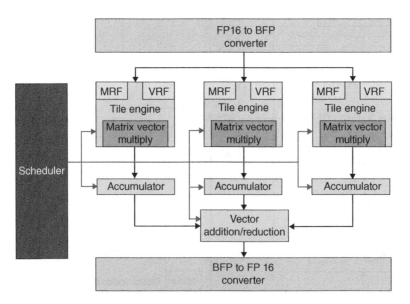

Figure 3.51 Matrix-vector multiplier overview.

accumulation tree through parallel lanes to achieve four dimensions of parallelism: inter MVM, MVM tiling, across the row of tile, and within the columns of the row (Figure 3.52).

Finally, the output of MVM is routed into vector MFU. The MFU supports the vector-vector operation, the addition and multiplication, the unary vector activation function (ReLU, sigmoid, and tanh). All MFUs are connected through the crossbar switches that multiple MFUs are chained together to support a longer sequence of the vector operation.

3.5.4 Hierarchical Decode and Dispatch (HDD)

The Catapult fabric employs a conventional scalar control processor to issue the instructions to the top-level scheduler dynamically. The scheduler decodes the instructions to the primitive operations that control the distributed computational resource parallel operation (Figure 3.53).

The scheduler dispatches to six decoders with four-level schemes. The top-level scheduler initializes MVM-specific instructions to second level one. It expands the operations for the target matrix with R rows and C columns. They are mapped into the matrix-vector tile engine with related pipeline register files, accumulator, and add-reduction unit for operation. Finally, it dispatches the control to start the computation with hundreds of dot-product engines.

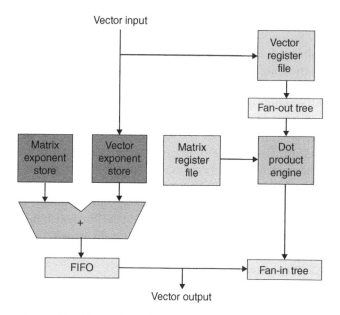

Figure 3.52   Tile engine architecture.

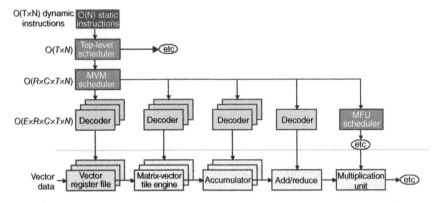

Figure 3.53 Hierarchical decode and dispatch scheme.

This architecture shows several important microarchitecture enhancements:

- Align the native vector dimension to model parameters for resource optimization during model evaluation
- Increase lane width to improve the intra-row parallelism
- Increase matrix multiply tiles to support large model parallelism

3.5.5 Sparse Matrix-Vector Multiplication

Microsoft also explores Sparse Matrix-Vector Multiplication (SMVM) [28] to improve overall performance through the Condensed Interleaved Sparse Representation (CISR) encoding format. Compared with the popular sparse matrix encoding scheme, Compressed Sparse Row (CSR) format, it stores only the nonzero matrix elements resulting in variable row size. It is difficult to control the various additions and reductions during parallel operations (Figure 3.54).

The Sparse Matrix-Vector Multiplier (SMVM) organizes the data into parallel channels where all row elements of the matrix are processed by the same channel. When the channel is exhausted, it fetches a new row for operation. Each channel initializes a new request to the high bandwidth Banked Vector Buffer (BVB) for a matrix fetch. It returns the input vector and corresponding matrix elements in channel FIFO for multiplication. The partial sums are fed to the fused accumulator for addition. After completing the row dot product, the results are sent to the output buffer. SMVM minimizes the communication and dependencies between the channels through CISR for parallel operations (Figure 3.55).

CSR format consists of three arrays: the first array lists all indexed nonzero elements in row-major order, the second array shows corresponding column index followed by the row-major order, and the last array is the row pointer to show the indexed column element starting position. The third array last entry shows the

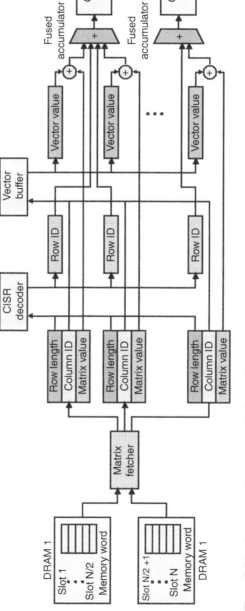

Figure 3.54 Sparse matrix-vector multiplier architecture.

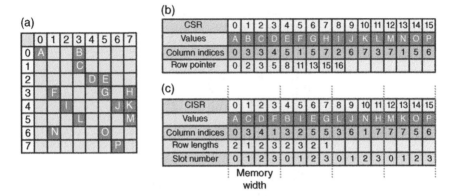

Figure 3.55 (a) Sparse Matrix; (b) CSR Format; and (c) CISR Format.

total number of nonzero elements. If the array contains the same pointer for two elements, it means that there is no zero between the two elements. This approach is difficult for parallel multiplication. An additional buffer is required to store intermediate data for parallel multiplication and the sequential decoding steps are used to determine the row boundaries.

CISR allows simple parallel multiplication hardware design. It applies four channel slots for data scheduling. The first nonzero elements (A, C, D, F) are placed in the first slots. The corresponding column indices are placed in the same order in the indices array. Once the row elements are exhausted, the next two row elements are assigned to the empty slots. The process is repeated until all nonzero elements are placed in the slots. The empty slots in the channel are filled with padding zero. The third array shows the row length. The static row scheduling is controlled by software that simplifies the hardware design.

For CISR decoding, the decoder first initializes the sequential row ID and sets the counter to the row length FIFO. The counter decrements every cycle and places the row ID in channel row ID FIFO for parallel multiplication. When the counter reaches zero, all the row IDs are processed, and the new row ID is assigned. The process repeats until the matrix row length array is exhausted and the matrix is fully decoded.

Exercise

1 Why does Intel choose mesh configuration over the ring network?

2 What are the advantages of the Intel new AXV-512 VNNI instruction set?

3 What is the enhancement of NVIDIA Turing Tensor Core?

4 How do you design NVIDIA NVLink2 transmitter and receiver?

5 How can you synthesize open-source NVDLA using FPGA approach?

6 What are the disadvantages of Google TPU systolic multiplier?

7 Why does Google change 256×256 MMU to 128×128 MXU?

8 Why does Microsoft choose a softcore approach for DNN accelerator implementation?

9 What is the advantage of CISR encoding over CSR?

10 Which is the best approach among Intel, Google, and Microsoft numerical precision format?

References

1 You, Y., Zhang, Z., Hsieh, C.-J. et al. (2018). ImageNet Training in Minutes. arXiv:1709.05011v10.

2 Rodriguez, A., Li, W., Dai, J. et al. (2017). Intel® Processors for Deep Learning Training. [Online]. Available: https://software.intel.com/en-us/articles/intel-processors-for-deep-learning-training.

3 Mulnix, D. (2017). Intel® Xeon® Processor Scalable Family Technical Overview. [Online]. Available: https://software.intel.com/en-us/articles/intel-xeon-processor-scalable-family-technical-overview.

4 Saletore, V., Karkada, D., Sripathi, V. et al. (2018). Boosting Deep Learning Training & Inference Performance on Intel Xeon and Intel Xeon Phi Processor. Intel.

5 (2019). Introduction to Intel Deep Learning Boost on Second Generation Intel Xeon Scalable Processors. [Online]. Available: https://software.intel.com/en-us/articles/introduction-to-intel-deep-learning-boost-on-second-generation-intel-xeon-scalable.

6 Rodriguez, A., Segal, E., Meiri, E. et al. (2018). Lower Numerical Precision Deep Learning Interence and Training. Intel.

7 (2018). Nvidia Turing GPU Architecture - Graphics Reinvented. Nvidia.

8 (2017). Nvidia Tesla P100 - The Most Advanced Datacenter Accelerator Ever Built Featuring Pascal GP100, the World's Fastest GPU. Nvidia.

9 (2017). Nvidia Tesla V100 GPU Architecture - The World's Most Advanced Data Center GPU. Nvidia.

10 Oh, N. (2018). The Nvidia Titan V Deep Leaering Deep Dive: It's All About Tensor Core. [Online].

11 Lavin, A. and Gray, S. (2016). Fast algorithms for convolutional neural networks. *2016 IEEE Conference on Computer Vision and Pattern Recognition (CVPR)*, 4013–4021.

12 Winograd, S. (1980). Arithmetic Complexity of Computations, Society for Industrial and Applied Mathematics (SIAM).

13 NVDLA Primer. [Online]. Available: http://nvdla.org/primer.html.

14 Farshchi, F., Huang, Q. and Yun, H. (2019). Integrating NVIDLA Deep Learning Accelerator (NVDLA) with RISC-V SoC on FireSim. arXiv:1903.06495v2.

15 Jouppi, N.P., Young, C., Patil, N. et al. (2017). In-Datacenter Performance Analysis of a Tensor Processing Unit. arXiv:1704.04760v1.

16 Jouppl, N.P., Young, C., Patil, N. et al. (2018). A Domain-Specific Architecture for Deep Neural Network. [Online].

17 Teich, P. (2018). Tearing Apart Google's TPU 3.0 AI Processor. [Online].

18 System Architecture. [Online]. Available: http://cloud.google.com/tpu/docs/system-architecture.

19 Kung, H. (1982). Why systolic architecture? *IEEE Computer* 15 (1): 37–46.

20 Kung, S. (1988). *VLSI Systolic Array Processors*. Prentice-Hall.

21 Dally, W. (2017). *High Performance Hardware for Machine Learning, Conference on Neural Information Processing Systems (NIPS) Tutorial.*

22 Williams, S., Waterman, A., and Patterson, D. (2009). Roofline: An insightful visual performance model for floating-point programs and multicore architecture. *Communications of the ACM* 52 (4): 65–76.

23 XLA (2017). TensorFlow, complied, Google Developers (6 March 2017) [online].

24 Putnam, A., Caulfield, A.M., Chung, E.S. et al. (2015). A reconfigurable fabric for accelerating large-scale datacenter services. *IEEE Micro* 35 (3): 10–22.

25 Caulfield, A.M., Chung, E.S., Putnam, A. et al. (2016). A cloud-scale acceleration architecture. *2016 49th Annual IEEE/ACM International Symposium on Microarchitecture (MICRO)*, pp. 1–13.

26 Fowers, J., Ovtcharov, K., Papamichael, M. et al. (2018). A configurable cloud-scale DNN processor for real-time AI. *ACM/IEEE 45th Annual Annual International Symposium on Computer Architecture (ISCA)*, 1–14.

27 Chung, E., Fowers, J., Ovtcharov, K. et al. (2018). Serving DNNs in real time at datacenter scale with project brainwave. *IEEE Micro* 38 (2): 8–20.

28 Fowers, J., Ovtcharov, K., Strauss, K. et al. (2014). A high memory bandwidth FPGA accelerator for sparse matrix-vector multiplication. *2014 IEEE 22nd Annual International Symposium on Field-Programmable Custom Computing Machines,* 36–43.

4

Streaming Graph Theory

Recently, graph-based deep-learning accelerators (Blaize GSP and Graphcore IPU) have been developed. They function as the Multiple Instructions Multiple Data (MIMD) machines to perform massive parallel operations. Graphcore IPU is also chosen by Microsoft and Dell for a deep learning accelerator in the next-generation datacenter.

4.1 Blaize Graph Streaming Processor

4.1.1 Stream Graph Model

Blaize Graph Streaming Processor (GSP) [1, 2] proposes the novel architecture based on Streaming Graph (GS) model [3] for deep learning applications. The streaming graph is widely applied to software development ranging from network traffic to database applications. It is targeted to process dynamic streaming data using a data stream model (TCS) with three important characteristics:

- Transit (T): Process massive graph streaming dynamically
- Compute (C): Perform a large amount of data in parallel
- Store (S): Store the data temporarily or archive it for long-term applications

Among the TCS models, the Turnstile model best describes the data behavior that the data arrives and departs from the stream dynamically. The model can be used for task scheduling.

With the input stream $a_1, a_2 \ldots$ arrives sequentially, it can be modeled as signal A where A is a one-dimensional function $[1 \cdots N] \rightarrow \mathrm{R}^2$

$$A_i \left[j \right] = A_{i-1} \left[j \right] + U_i \tag{4.1}$$

Artificial Intelligence Hardware Design: Challenges and Solutions, First Edition.
Albert Chun Chen Liu and Oscar Ming Kin Law.
© 2021 The Institute of Electrical and Electronics Engineers, Inc. Published 2021
by John Wiley & Sons, Inc.

where

a_i is the input data $a_i = (j, U_i)$ and updates the signal $A[j]$

A_i is the signal after ith item in the stream

U_i may be positive or negative to indicate the signal arrival or departure

During the stream, it measures signal A with the functions:

- Process time per item a_i in the stream (Process)
- Computing time for A (Compute)
- Storage space of A_t at time t (Storage) (Figure 4.1)

Currently, the research focuses on streaming graph algorithms [4] and different partitions [5] to enhance the overall efficiency.

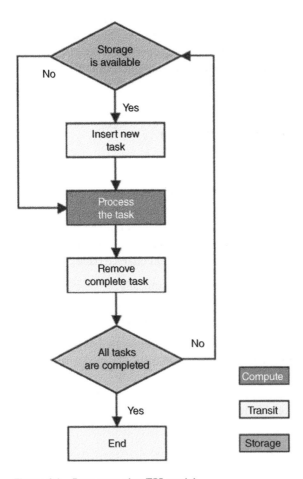

Figure 4.1 Data streaming TCS model.

4.1.2   Depth First Scheduling Approach

Blaize GSP transforms the neural network model into the Direct Acyclic Graph (DAG) format (*V*, *E*) where *V* is the vertex representing the Processing Element (PE) and *E* is the edge for the weighted connection between the PEs. The Depth First Scheduling (DFS) is applied to schedule the operations. It first visits the vertex in the left tree until the last node. Then, it goes back to visit the vertex in the right one. The action repeats until all the vertices are visited. It records the visit order and the task schedule is the reverse of the visit order. This approach allows GSP to schedule the operation as soon as the data is available. It enables the dynamic graph execution and supports the sparse and conditional graph (Figure 4.2).

The GSP achieves four-level parallelism in architectural design:

- Task Parallelism (direct graph processing): Multiple layer nodes can be processed in parallel when the data is available. It is independent of other nodes with a dynamic schedule
- Thread Parallelism (fine grain thread scheduling): Each processor supports multiple threads per cycle. The changing context is achieved through thread switch or new thread launch
- Data Parallelism (2D data block processing): Unaligned data block can be operated through special instruction, data block move/add, and dot product multiplication
- Instruction Parallelism (hardware instruction scheduling): Each processor schedules the instructions when their dependencies are fulfilled. Then it executes the instruction in parallel

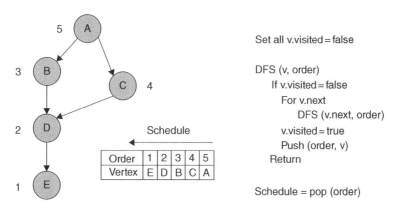

Figure 4.2   Blaize depth-first scheduling approach.

4.1.3 Graph Streaming Processor Architecture

The GSP architecture consists of System Controller, Direct Memory Access (DMA) Unit, Command Unit, Graph Scheduler, Execution Tile, Graph Streaming Processor, Special Math, Data Cache, and Memory Management Unit (MMU) (Figures 4.3–4.6).

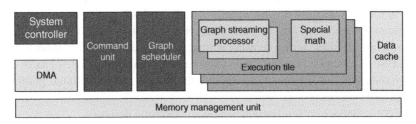

Figure 4.3 Blaize graph streaming processor architecture.

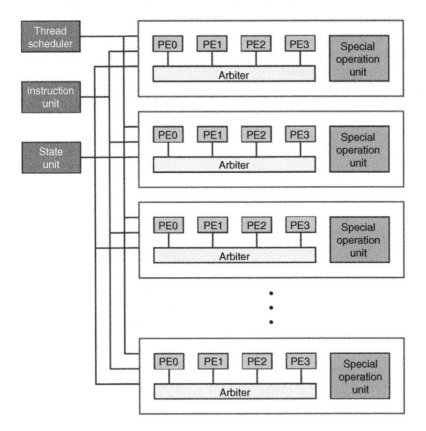

Figure 4.4 Blaize GSP thread scheduling.

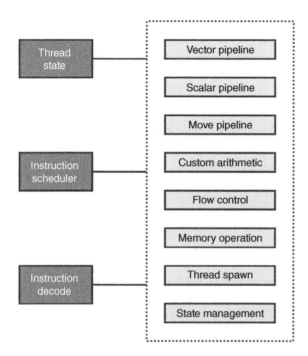

Figure 4.5 Blaize GSP instruction scheduling.

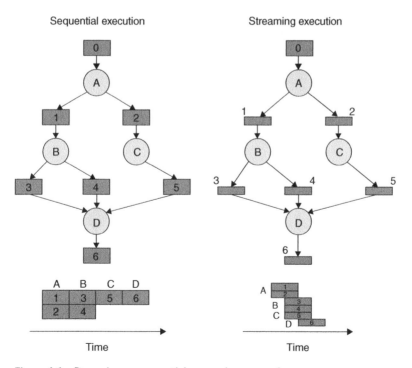

Figure 4.6 Streaming vs. sequential processing comparison.

Compare streaming against sequential processing with several benefits.
Sequential Processing

- Commonly used by Graphics Processing Unit (GPU) and Digital Signal Processor (DSP)
- Data access between intermediate buffer and DRAM memory is not globally cacheable
- Excessive latency and power for memory access
- Data transfer after the task is completed
- Require large data storage

Streaming Processing

- Small intermediate buffer for local processing
- Cached data is easily supported
- Memory bandwidth is reduced to improve the performance with less power
- Support both task and data-parallel processing
- Data is sent to the next node when it is ready (Figure 4.7)

For a general neural network, it processes the node one at a time without taking the node relationship into consideration. A large amount of data is stored in memory resulting in bandwidth and power issues. With the graph streaming approach, the GSP schedules the operation when the data is ready without waiting for other data. It improves the overall performance with less memory access. For convolution, it first multiplies the filter weight with the input feature map. Then starts the addition between the partial sum S and the bias B, resulting in the final Y.

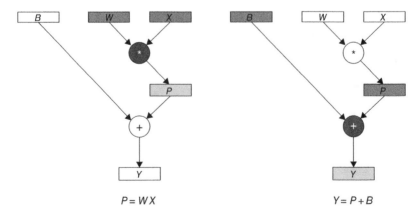

$$P = WX$$

$$Y = P + B$$

$$Y = WX + B$$

Figure 4.7 Blaize GSP convolution operation.

4.2   Graphcore Intelligence Processing Unit

Graphcore develops Intelligence Processing Unit (IPU) [6–9] which adopts a similar approach as Blaize GSP that applies the graph theory to perform the fine-grained operation with a massive parallel thread for deep learning applications. It offers Multiple Instruction Multiple Data (MIMD) parallelism with distributive local memory.

4.2.1   Intelligence Processor Unit Architecture

Each IPU consists of 1216 Processing Elements (PEs) called tiles. The PE contains the computational unit and 256 kb local memory. There is no additional memory storage, except the register file. An on-chip interconnect called exchange provides high bandwidth and low-latency communication among the tiles. The high-speed IPU link connects all the IPU processors together.

Similar to Nvidia Simultaneous Multithreading (SMT), IPU offers six individual processing threads on smaller data blocks with irregular data pattern. Each thread supports distinct instruction and execution flow without performance penalty. It avoids the pipeline stalls, hides the instruction latency, and increases throughput. Each tile rotates among threads according to a static round-robin schedule (Figure 4.8).

4.2.2   Accumulating Matrix Product (AMP) Unit

IPU employs a specialized pipelined structure Accumulating Matrix Product (AMP) unit which computes 64 bits mixed-precision or 16 bits single-precision floating-point operation per clock cycle. IPU adapts distributed local memory to support computation with lower latency (Figures 4.9 and 4.10).

4.2.3   Memory Architecture

IPU tile contains 256 kb local memory and total 304 Mb memory for the entire processor. Each tile has 21 bits address space shared by six execution units for local computation. The local scratchpad offers aggregate bandwidth of 45 Tb/s with six clock cycle latency.

4.2.4   Interconnect Architecture

Multi-IPUs are connected through the IPU link. It offers computational power and memory resource for large neural network model processing. Two IPUs are connected through three IPU links with bidirectional bandwidth 65 Gb/s each

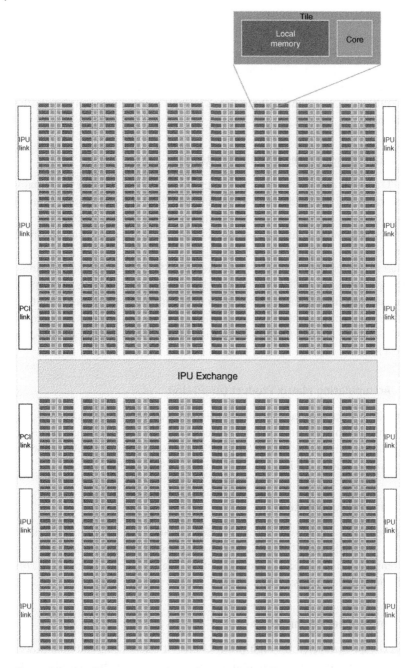

Figure 4.8 Intelligence processing unit architecture [8].

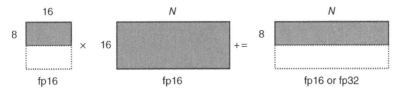

Figure 4.9 Intelligence processing unit mixed-precision multiplication.

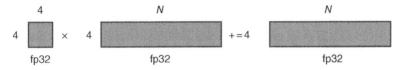

Figure 4.10 Intelligence processing unit single-precision multiplication.

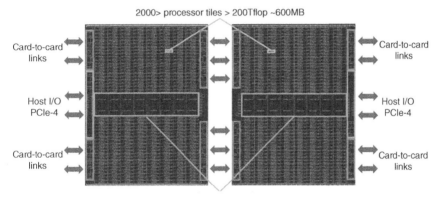

Figure 4.11 Intelligence processing unit interconnect architecture [9].

and two links are reserved for intra-band transfer. It connects to the host through the PCIe-4 link (Figure 4.11).

4.2.5 Bulk Synchronous Parallel Model

The operation of IPU is based on Bulk Synchronous Parallel (BSP) model [10, 11] (Figure 4.12). It divides the operation into the local computation phase, communication phase, and barrier synchronization.

- Computation Phase: Every process performs computation with local memory without any communication among the processes.
- Communication Phase: Each process exchanges the information with the target process without any computation.

● Barrier Synchronization: No process moves to the next phase until all processes reach the barrier. Neither computation nor communication occurs in this phase.

IPU executes the BSP model where the instructions are sent to the core before the computation starts. The cores perform the computation with local memory only. It communicates with the target after the computation is completed. All the cores are synchronized through barrier synchronization (Figures 4.13 and 4.14).

Blaize GSP and Graphcore IPU are good solutions for cloud-based applications. They can handle the massively parallel operations through distributive processors. However, they are not suitable for embedded inference applications due to area and power criteria. Therefore, various deep learning accelerators are introduced to address these limitations.

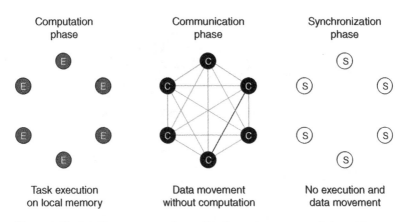

Figure 4.12   Intelligence processing unit bulk synchronous parallel model.

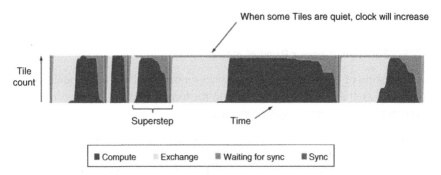

Figure 4.13   Intelligence processing unit bulk synchronous parallel execution trace [9].

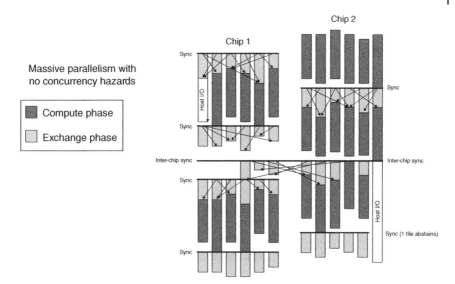

Figure 4.14 Intelligence processing unit bulk synchronous parallel inter-chip execution [9].

Exercise

1 What is the difference between a Single Instruction Multiple Data (SIMD) machine and Multiple Instructions Multiple Data (MIMD) machine?

2 What is the data streaming TCS model?

3 Why does Blaize choose Depth First (DF) rather than Breadth-First (BS) scheduling approach?

4 Why is Graphcore IPU suitable for data center application?

5 Why is the Bulk Synchronous Parallel (BSP) model important for Graphcore IPU?

6 What are the advantages of the graph streaming DNN processor over CPU and GPU?

7 What are the disadvantages of the graph streaming DNN processor?

References

1 Chung, E., Fowers, J., Ovtcharov, K. et al. (2018). Serving DNNs in real time at datacenter scale with project brainwave. *IEEE Micro* 38 (2): 8–20.

2 Fowers, J., Ovtcharov, K., Strauss, K., et al. (2014). A high memory bandwidth FPGA accelerator for sparse matrix-vector multiplication. *IEEE 22nd Annual International Symposium on Field-Programmable Custom Computing Machines,* 36–43.

3 Blaize. Blaize graph streaming processor: the revolutionary graph-native architecture. White paper, Blaize [Online].

4 Blaize. Blaize Picasso software development platform for graph streaming processor (GSP): graph-native software platform. White Paper, Blaize [Online].

5 Muthukrishnan, S. (2015). Data streams: algorithm and applications. *Foundations and Trends in Theoretical Computer Science* 1 (2): 117–236.

6 McGregor, A. (2014). Graph stream algorithms: a survey. *ACM SIGMOD Record* 43 (1): 9–20.

7 Abbas, Z., Kalavri, V., Cabone, P., and Vlassov, V. (2018). Streaming graph partitioning: an experimental study. *Proceedings of the VLDB Endowment* 11 (11): 1590–1603.

8 Cook, V.G., Koneru, S., Yin, K., and Munagala, D. (2017). Graph streaming processor: a next-generation computing architecture. In: *Hot Chip*. HC29.21.

9 Knowles, S. (2017). Scalable silicon compute. *Workshop on Deep Learning at Supercomputer Scale.*

10 Jia, Z., Tillman, B., Maggioni, M., and Scarpazza, D.P. (2019). Dissecting the Graphcore IPU. arXiv:1912.03413v1.

11 NIPS (2017). *Graphcore – Intelligence Processing Unit. NIPS.*

5

Convolution Optimization

The convolution is the computation-intensive operation that occupies more than 90% of resource, the reuse strategy (feature maps reuse, filter weights reuse, and partial sum reuse) is proposed to minimize the data access for performance improvement. The data-streaming flow with filter decomposition technique and row stationary (RS) flow is used to illustrate the reuse approaches.

5.1 Deep Convolutional Neural Network Accelerator

Besides the cloud-based deep learning accelerator, custom hardware is developed for embedded deep learning applications. University of California, Los Angeles (UCLA) introduces Deep Convolutional Neural Network (DCNN) accelerator [1, 2] using 65 nm technology with 5 mm^2 die area. It achieves 152 GOPS peak throughput and 434 GOPS/W energy efficiency at 350 mW power consumption. It highlights the key features as follows:

- Streaming data flow minimizes data access with high energy efficiency
- Interleaving architecture enables multiple features parallel computation without memory bandwidth increase
- Large-size filter decomposition supports arbitrary convolution window, the accelerator is highly reconfigurable without extra hardware penalty
- Reduce the main Convolution Unit (CU) workload through additional parallel pooling functional unit

Artificial Intelligence Hardware Design: Challenges and Solutions, First Edition.
Albert Chun Chen Liu and Oscar Ming Kin Law.
© 2021 The Institute of Electrical and Electronics Engineers, Inc. Published 2021
by John Wiley & Sons, Inc.

5.1.1 System Architecture

The DCNN accelerator consists of the buffer bank, the Column (COL) buffer, the Accumulation (ACCU) buffer, the Convolution Unit (CU), and the instruction decoder. The buffer bank stores the intermediate data and exchanges the data between the external memory. It is divided into two sets of buffers targeted for input and output data. The buffer bank is further split into Bank A and Bank B to store odd and even channels/features, respectively. The COL buffer remaps the buffer bank output to the inputs of the CU engine. The CU engine is composed of 16 convolution units and each supports the convolution with a kernel size of up to three. All the operations are done using 16 bits fixed-point format to speed up the operation with less memory access. A local prefetch unit fetches the data from the Direct Memory Access (DMA) controller periodically and updates the weight and bias values in the engine. Finally, the ACCU buffer with scratchpad is implemented to accumulate the partial sums during the convolution. A separate max-pooling functional unit is embedded in the ACCU buffer to reduce the CU engine workload (Figure 5.1).

The control commands are stored in external memory. They are loaded into a 128-depth command FIFO to enable the accelerator. The commands are divided into configuration and execution commands. The configuration commands configure the network layer and enable pooling and ReLU functions. The execution commands initialize the convolution/pooling and instruct how to decompose the filter (Figure 5.2).

During the convolution, the input feature maps are loaded into the CU engine sequentially and the engine computes the data with corresponding filter weights.

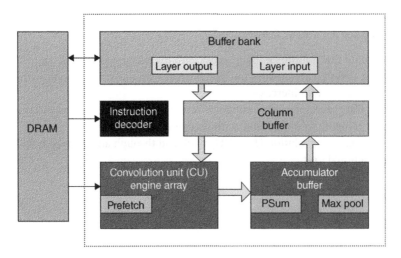

Figure 5.1 Deep convolutional neural network hardware architecture.

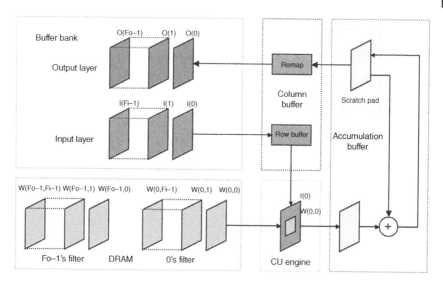

Figure 5.2 Convolution computation.

The results are sent to the ACCU buffer and accumulated in the scratchpad. The accelerator repeats the process with the next filter weights until all the input feature maps are computed.

5.1.2 Filter Decomposition

To support different filter kernel size, a filter decomposition technique is proposed to map large kernel size convolution through a smaller (3×3) CU engine to simplify the hardware design. If the original kernel size is not a multiple of three, zero-padding weights are added into the kernel boundary. The extended filter with zero-padding outputs the same result as the original one during computation (Figure 5.3).

The extended filter is decomposed into multiple 3×3 filters. Each filter is assigned a shifted address based on the original filter top left position. For example, 5×5 filter is decomposed into four 3×3 filters where one zero-padding row and column are added in original filter with shift address F0 (0, 0), F1 (0, 3), F2 (3, 0), and F3 (3, 3). After the convolution, the results are recombined into one output feature map (Figure 5.4).

The output feature map with shifted address is defined as

$$I_o\left(X,Y\right)=\sum_i I_{di}\left(X+x_i,Y+y_i\right) \tag{5.1}$$

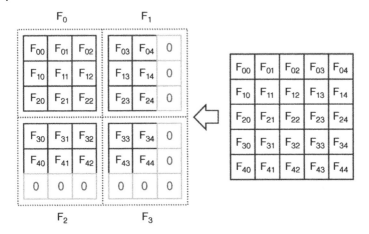

Figure 5.3 Filter decomposition with zero padding.

where

I_o is the output image

I_{di} is the ith decomposed filter output images

(X, Y) is the current output address

(x_i, y_i) is the ith decomposed filter shift address

The filter decomposition is derived from the equations:

$$F_{3k}\left(a, b\right) = \sum_{i=0}^{3K-1} f\left(i, j\right) \times I_i\left(a+i, b+j\right)$$

$$F_{3k}\left(a, b\right) = \sum_{i=0}^{K-1}\sum_{j=0}^{K-1}\sum_{l=0}^{2}\sum_{m=0}^{2} f\left(3i+l, 3j+m\right) \times I_i\left(a+3i+l, b+3j+m\right)$$

$$F_{3k}\left(a, b\right) = \sum_{i=0}^{K-1}\sum_{j=0}^{K-1} F_{3ij}\left(a+3i, b+3j\right) \tag{5.2}$$

$$F_{3ij}\left(a, b\right) = \sum_{m=0}^{2}\sum_{l=0}^{2} f\left(3i+l, 3j+m\right) \times I_i\left(a+3i+l, b+3j+m\right)$$

$$0 \le i < K-1, 0 \le k < K-1 \tag{5.3}$$

where

$F_{3k}(a, b)$ is a filter with kernel size $3K$

$f(i, j)$ is the filter and (i, j) is the weight relative position

$I_i(a+3i+l, b+3j+m)$ is the image pixel position

F_{3ij} is K^2 different 3×3 kernel size filter

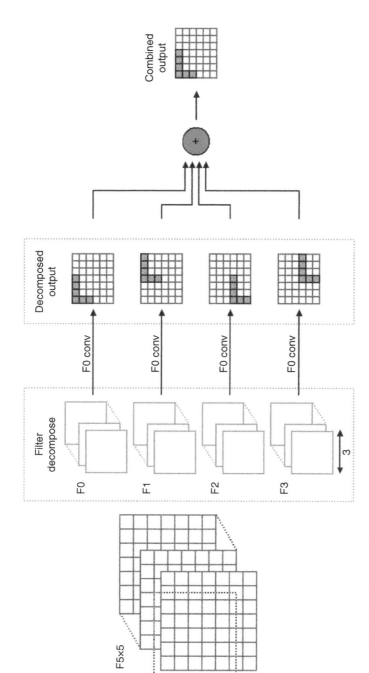

Figure 5.4 Filter decomposition approach.

Therefore, $3K \times 3K$ filter can be decomposed into K^2 different 3×3 filter for computation without accuracy loss.

The filter decomposition maximizes the hardware resource usage with zero-padding penalty. The overall efficiency can be calculated:

$$Efficiency \; loss = \frac{Zero - padding \; MAC}{Total \; MAC} \qquad (5.4)$$

Based on different neural network model comparison, the decomposition filter approach benefits small size filter (Table 5.1).

5.1.3 Streaming Architecture

To minimize the data movement, the streaming architecture is proposed with filter weights and input feature maps reuse strategy:

- The filter weights are reused for whole input features
- The input feature maps are reused to generate the output features

5.1.3.1 Filter Weights Reuse

During 3×3 convolution, the filter weights are stored in the CU engine and the input feature maps are fed into the CU engine and perform the dot product computation, the output partial sums are stored in ACCU buffer for future accumulation. The filter weights are not updated until all input feature maps are computed. For 1×1 convolution, a similar approach is adopted where the seven out of nine multipliers are turned off. Two multipliers are used to calculate the odd and even channel partial sums simultaneously to speed up the entire operations. The data streaming flow is realized through the movement of the filter weights. The filter weights interact with the input feature maps to perform the convolution. Sixteen 3×3 filter windows process multiple row data in parallel to simplify the hardware design (Figure 5.5).

Table 5.1 Efficiency loss comparison.

Model	Kernel size	Efficiency loss (%)
AlexNet	3–11	13.74
ResNet-18	1–7	1.64
ResNet-50	1–7	0.12
Inception v3	1–5	0.89

To maximize the buffer bank output bandwidth, the sixteen rows of data are divided into two sets, odd number channel data set and even ones. Two FIFO buffer is paired with each data set and transferred eight input rows to ten overlapping output rows. It enables eight 3×3 CU engine to run in parallel with overlapped data to improve the overall performance (Figure 5.6).

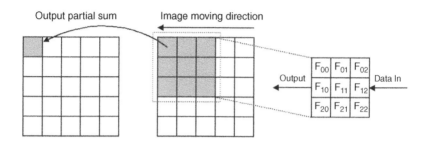

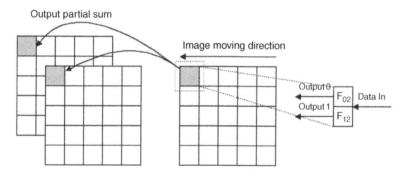

Figure 5.5 Data streaming architecture with the data flow.

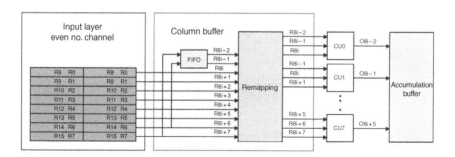

Figure 5.6 DCNN accelerator COL buffer architecture.

5.1.3.2 Input Channel Reuse

To utilize CU engine resource for 1×1 convolution, an interleaved architecture is proposed to separate the sixteen data set into the odd and even number channel data sets. Two data sets are multiplied with two different filter weights to produce 32 outputs through the CU engine, the summation function combines the same partial sums to generate the correct result. The data bandwidth is reduced by half for each channel data set but the final output is the same as input bandwidth due to odd/even channel implementations. X (O, 0) to X (O, 7) represents the odd number channel inputs and X (E, 0) to X (E, 7) referred to the even ones. O (0, 1) to O (0, 7) and E (0, 1) to E (0, 7) are the output partial sums from odd/even number channels (Figure 5.7).

5.1.4 Pooling

The pooling function can be separated into average and max pooling and constructed differently in the DCNN accelerator.

5.1.4.1 Average Pooling

The average pooling can be implemented using a CU engine where the input/output channel sizes are equal in the convolutional layer. The kernel size matches with the pooling windows. The corresponding filter weights are set to $1/K^2$ and all others are set to zero. It transforms the convolution to theaverage pooling function.

$$O\big[io\big]\big[r\big]\big[c\big] = \sum_{ii=0}^{l} \sum_{i=0}^{K-1}\sum_{j=0}^{K-1} I\big[io\big]\big[ii\big]\big[r+i\big]\big[c+j\big] \times W\big[io\big]\big[ii\big]\big[i\big]\big[j\big]$$

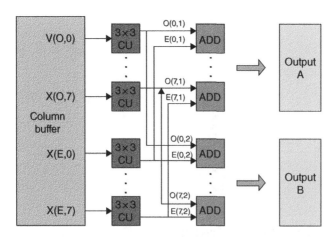

Figure 5.7 Data streaming architecture with 1×1 convolution mode.

$$W\big[io\big]\big[ii\big]\big[i\big]\big[j\big]=\begin{cases}\dfrac{1}{K^2} & \text{if } ii=io\\[2mm]0 & \text{if } ii\neq io\end{cases} \tag{5.5}$$

where

ii is the input channel number

io is the output channel number

(r, c) is the output feature row and column position

W is the filter weight matrix

K is the average pooling window size

5.1.4.2 Max Pooling

The max-pooling is implemented as a separate module within the ACCU buffer. The module connects to the scratchpad with eight rows from one output feature. The eight row data shares the same column address to be accessed in parallel. To support different convolution stride and pooling size, a multiplexer is used to select the input data to the corresponding scratchpad. The max-pooling unit is implemented using four-input comparators with the register to store intermediate results. It takes three-input data and one max value from the previous cycle for comparison. The max-pooling result is fed back to the comparator for the next comparison until all input data is exhausted. It outputs the final max-pooling result (Figure 5.8).

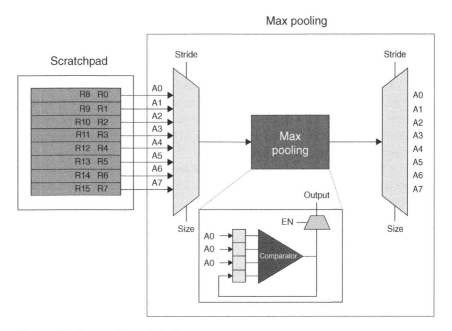

Figure 5.8   Max pooling architecture.

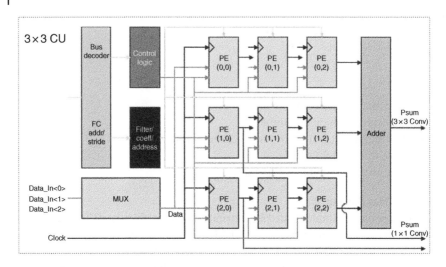

Figure 5.9 Convolution engine architecture.

5.1.5 Convolution Unit (CU) Engine

The 3 × 3 Convolution Unit (CU) engine consists of nine processing elements (PEs) with an adder to combine all the output results (Figure 5.9). The PE performs the multiplication between the input feature maps and the filter weights, the partial sums are fed to the adder for summation. It passes the input feature maps to the next PE for processing. To support different convolution window size, the PEs can be turned on/off by a control signal for power saving.

For 3 × 3 convolution, the filter weights are fetched from external memory and stored in CU engine through a global bus. The multiplication result is sent to adder for summation and delivered to output feature maps. After the current input feature maps are exhausted, it signals the CU to update the filter weights for next input feature maps computation.

For 1 × 1 convolution, only (1, 0) and (2, 0) PE are used to compute the odd/even number data set and directly output the results. The other adders are turned off to save power.

5.1.6 Accumulation (ACCU) Buffer

Accumulation (ACCU) buffer accumulates the partial sums and stores output feature maps in the scratchpad. ACCU buffer consists of ping-pong buffer for the partial product accumulation, temporary storage for max-pooling, and a readout block for output (Figure 5.10). During the convolution, only one buffer points to

Figure 5.10 Accumulation (ACCU) buffer architecture.

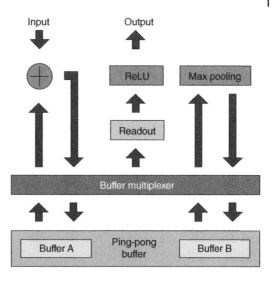

the accumulator to process convolution results, the other buffer connects to pooling blocks for pooling operation. When the accumulation is completed, it switches the buffer to perform pooling operation and others start the next partial summation.

5.1.7 Model Compression

Model compression technique [3] is adopted to optimize the convolution. It trains the neural network model, then prunes the zero connections and the others below the threshold. It clusters the filter weights and generates the quantized codebook. After that, it applies the Huffman encoding to achieve 39×–49× compression ratio for size reduction (Figure 5.11).

5.1.8 System Performance

UCLA accelerator performs the deep learning inference operations using 16 bits fixed-point arithmetic with 300 mW power dissipation at 500 MHz. The peak throughput reaches 152 GOPS with high energy efficiency at 434 GOPs/W. The performance comparison among other deep learning accelerators[1] is shown in the Table 5.2.

---

1 Stanford EIE accelerator in Section 8.1 and MIT Eyeriss accelerator in Section 5.2.

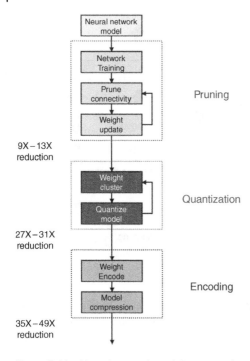

Figure 5.11 Neural network model compression.

Table 5.2 DNN accelerator performance comparison.

	UCLA DCNN accelerator	Stanford EIE accelerator	MIT Eyeriss accelerator
Core area	$5\,mm^2$	$12\,mm^2$	$16\,mm^2$
Technology	65 nm	65 nm	65 nm
Gate count	1.3 M	1.2 M	3.2 M
Supply voltage	1 V	0.82 V–1.17 V	1.2 V
Peak throughput	154 GOPS	84 GOPS	64 GOPS
Energy efficiency	434 GOPS/W	166 GOPS/W	1.4 TOPS/w
Precision	16 bits	16 bits	16 bits
Max pooling	Yes	No	Yes
Average pooling	Yes	No	No

5.2   Eyeriss Accelerator

To resolve the deep learning convolution bottleneck, Massachusetts Institute of Technology (MIT) Eyeriss accelerator [4,5] proposes Row Stationary (RS) dataflow to reconfigure the spatial architecture to minimize data access with the following key features:

- Develop novel spatial architecture with sequential processing configuration
- Implement Row Stationary (RS) dataflow to exploit the data pattern to minimize memory access
- Support four-level memory hierarchy to resolve memory bottleneck. It fully utilizes the PE scratchpad (spad) and inter-PE communication; it also minimizes the Global Buffer (GLB) and external memory data transfer
- Support the point-to-point and multicast Network-on-Chip (NoC) architecture
- Employ Run-Length Compression (RLC) format to eliminate the ineffectual zero operation

5.2.1   Eyeriss System Architecture

Eyeriss accelerator partitions the system into two clock domains, the data processing core clock and communication link clock. The core clock controls the 12×14 PE array, the global buffer, RLC codec, and ReLU unit. It allows the PE to perform the computation using the local scratchpad or communicate with its neighbor PEs or the GLB through the NoC. The system supports a four-level memory hierarchy, the data transfer between the GLB and external memory through asynchronous FIFO, the data exchange between the PE and GLB using the NoC, and the communication between the ReLU and RLC codec as well as the local temporary data storage using scratchpad. With the separate control, the PE can run independently with other PEs under the same core clock. The link clock controls the data transfer between the external memory through 64 bits bidirectional data bus (Figure 5.12).

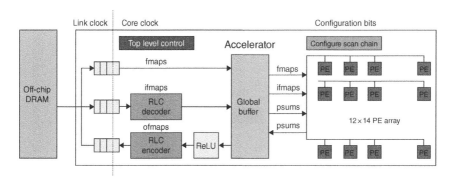

Figure 5.12   Eyeriss system architecture.

Eyeriss accelerator processes the convolutional neural network layer by layer. It first configures the PE array based on the layer function and its size, then performs the mapping and decides the transfer pattern. The input feature maps (ifmaps) and the filter maps (fmaps) are loaded from the external memory into the PE for computation. The output feature maps (ofmaps) are written back into the external memory after the computation is completed.

5.2.2   2D Convolution to 1D Multiplication

In order to utilize the hardware resource, it maps 2D convolution to 1D vector multiplication. It converts 2D fmaps into 1D vector and changes the 2D ifmaps to Toeplitz matrix. After that, it performs fmaps vector and ifmaps matrix multiplication to generate the partial sums (psums). The psums are accumulated to generate the ofmaps. After the multiplication is completed, it rearranges the output vector into the 2D matrix. This approach can be further extended to multiple channel operations (Figure 5.13).

To demonstrate 2D convolution to 1D vector multiplication, 2×2 fmaps convolves with 3×3 ifmaps to create ofmaps. It rearranges fmaps as a 1D vector and changes ifmaps to Toeplitz matrix. Then it performs the dot product to create a 1D output vector. The output vector is reordered to generate 2D ofmaps. The entire operations are illustrated as follows (Figure 5.14):

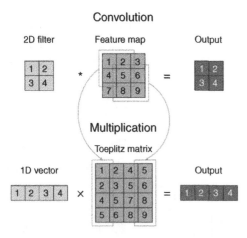

Figure 5.13   2D convolution to 1D multiplication mapping.

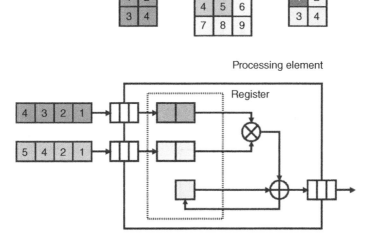

Figure 5.14 2D convolution to 1D multiplication – step #1.

The first two elements of both fmaps and corresponding ifmaps are loaded into the spad and performs multiplication to create the psums and are stored in local spads for the next multiplication (Figure 5.15).

The next two elements are loaded to PE for multiplication again and accumulated with the stored psums (Figure 5.16).

Until all the elements are exhausted for the multiplication, the PE outputs the result to ofmaps. The same fmaps and next ifmaps are loaded into the spads to start new multiplication (Figure 5.17).

5.2.3 Stationary Dataflow

In order to improve energy efficiency, the data movement is reduced through data stationary approaches. It stores the data locally for reuse. It is further divided into three categories – Output Stationary (OS), Weight Stationary (WS) and Input Stationary (IS).

5.2.3.1 Output Stationary

The Output Stationary (OS) targets to minimize the psums read/write access through the local accumulation for energy saving. Multiple ifmaps and fmaps are fed into the accumulators for computation. They are also transferred spatially across the PE for further processing. The accumulator is easy to modify to support

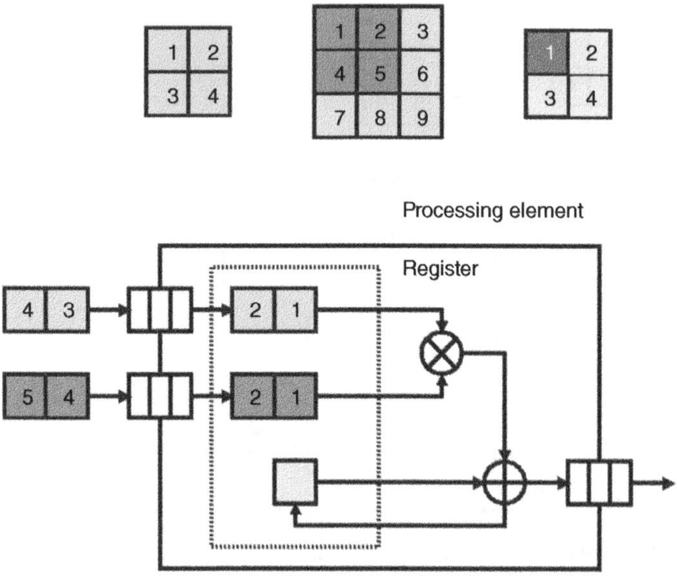

Figure 5.15 2D convolution to 1D multiplication – step #2.

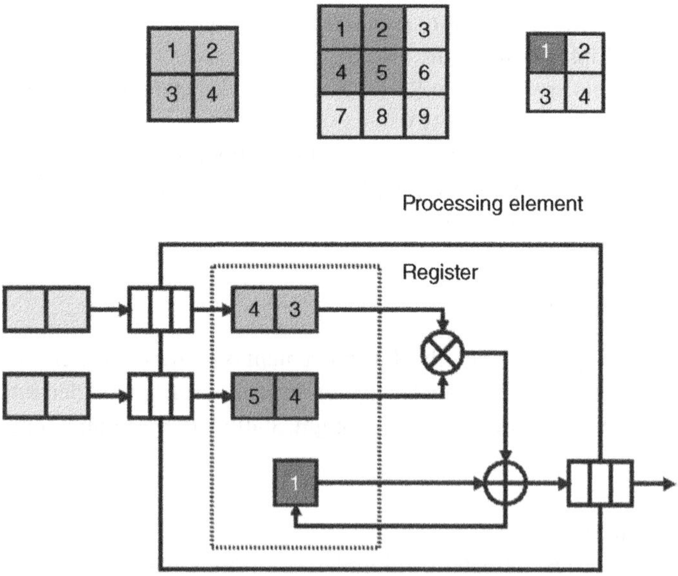

Figure 5.16 2D convolution to 1D multiplication – step #3.

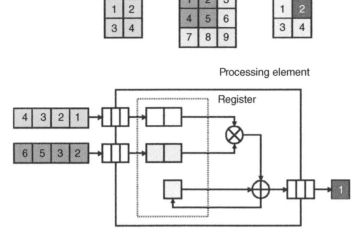

Figure 5.17 2D convolution to 1D multiplication – step #4.

the output stationary. From the index looping,[2] the output index stays constant until the multiplication between the ifmaps and fmaps are exhausted (Figures 5.18 and 5.19).

5.2.3.2 Weight Stationary

The Weight Stationary (WS) stores the fmaps in the local buffer to minimize the read access. It maximizes the convolution efficiency through fmaps reuse. It broadcasts the ifmaps and psums spatially across the PE array. Using the index looping, the weight index keeps constant and performs effective multiplications (Figures 5.20 and 5.21).

5.2.3.3 Input Stationary

The Input Stationary (IS) reuses the ifmaps locally for convolution and minimizes the read access. It unicasts the fmaps and accumulated psums spatially across the PE array. However, the reuse efficiency is not as good as other stationary approaches. The major drawback of input stationary takes more cycle to complete the convolution (Figures 5.22 and 5.23).

---

2 For index looping, $O = 9$, $I = 12$, $W = 4$.

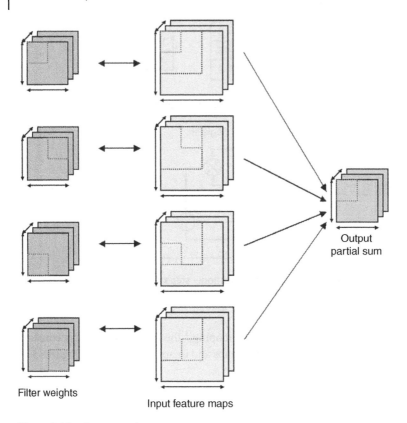

Figure 5.18 Output stationary.

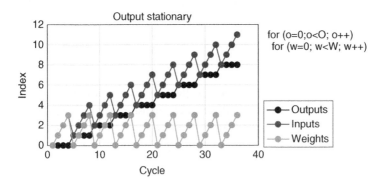

Figure 5.19 Output stationary index looping.

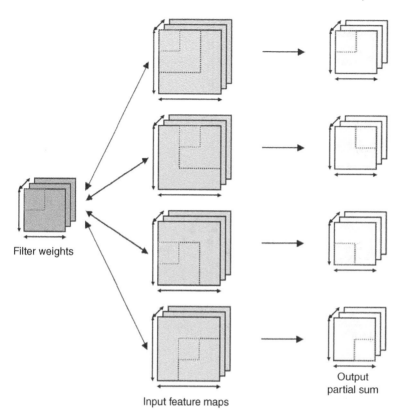

Figure 5.20 Weight stationary.

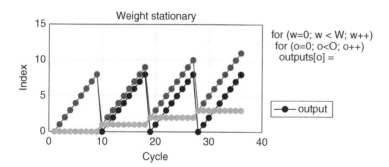

Figure 5.21 Weight stationary index looping.

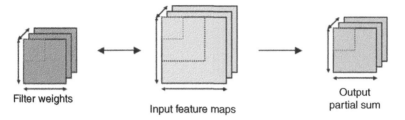

Filter weights

Input feature maps

Output partial sum

Figure 5.22 Input stationary.

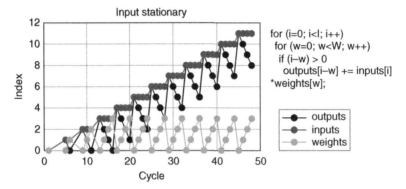

Input stationary

```
for (i=0; i<I; i++)
  for (w=0; w<W; w++)
    if (i–w) > 0
      outputs[i–w] += inputs[i]
        *weights[w];
```

- outputs
- inputs
- weights

Figure 5.23 Input stationary index looping.

5.2.4 Row Stationary (RS) Dataflow

To perform 2D convolution using 1D multiplication, it applies Row Stationary (RS) dataflow to optimize data movement (Figure 5.24):

- Row of feature maps (fmaps) are reused across PEs horizontally
- Row of input feature maps (ifmaps) are reused across PEs diagonally
- Row of partial sums (psums) are reused across PEs vertically

With the RS dataflow, the data is stored within the PEs for computation. It minimizes the data movement between the global buffer and external memory. Through the time-interleaved approach, the fmaps and ifmaps are reused for computation in the same clock cycle. Until the operation is completed, the psums result is sent to the neighbor PEs for the next operation. Data reuse and local accumulation significantly reduce the memory access for energy saving.

5.2.4.1 Filter Reuse

For filter reuse, the fmaps are loaded from the external memory into the spads and stay constant for the same set of ifmaps. Multiple ifmaps are loaded into PE spads and concatenated together. Each PE performs 1D multiplication between the

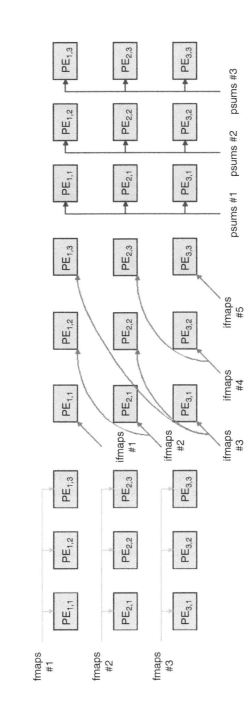

Figure 5.24 Eyeriss Row Stationary (RS) dataflow.

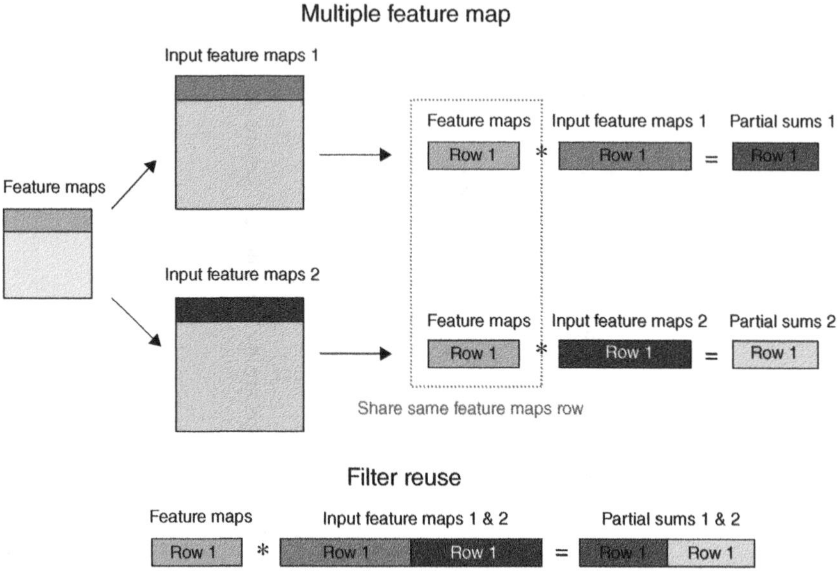

Figure 5.25 Filter reuse.

ifmaps and same fmaps to generate the psums. The psums are stored in PE spads for further computation. It minimizes the fmaps data movement for energy reduction (Figure 5.25).

5.2.4.2 Input Feature Maps Reuse

For input feature maps reuse, the ifmaps are first loaded into the PE spad, the two fmaps are time-interleaved. Each PE performs 1D multiplication between the two fmaps with the same ifmaps. It speeds up the overall operation. However, the drawback of this approach is the large spads size requirement for both fmaps and psums to support time-interleaved operations (Figure 5.26).

5.2.4.3 Partial Sums Reuse

For partial sums reuse, both fmaps and ifmaps are loaded into the PE, both are time-interleaved. Each PE performs 1D multiplication between the corresponding fmaps and ifmaps. The psums are accumulated for the same channel. Similarly, both ifmaps and fmaps spads size are increased to support the partial sum reuse strategy (Figure 5.27).

5.2.5 Run-Length Compression (RLC)

Since the ReLU module sets all the negative results to zero, it introduces sparsity into the network. To avoid the ineffectual zero computation, Eyeriss accelerator adopts the Run-Length Compression (RLC) format to encode nonzero elements to

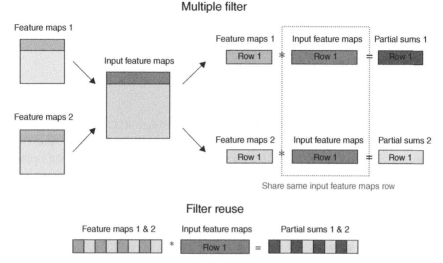

Figure 5.26 Feature map reuse.

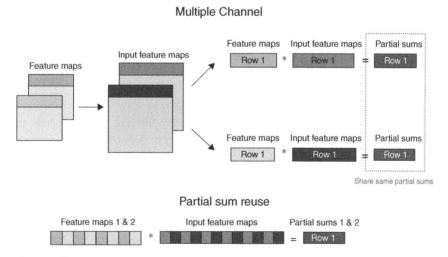

Figure 5.27 Partial sum reuse.

resolve the memory bottleneck. The data is stored in 64 bits RLC format with three pairs of Runs and Levels. five bits Run represents the max number of 31 consecutive zeros followed by 16 bits Level to store the nonzero data. The last bit indicates if the word is the last one in the code (Figure 5.28).

Except for the first-layer ifmaps, all the fmaps and ifmaps are encoded using RLC format and stored in the external memory. The accelerator reads the encoded

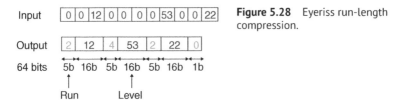

Figure 5.28 Eyeriss run-length compression.

ifmaps from external memory and decodes them through RLC decoder. After the convolution, the results pass through ReLU layer to generate the zero data. The data are compressed using the RLC encoder to remove ineffectual zero and stored the nonzero elements in RLC format. Finally, the encoded data is written back to external memory. This approach introduces 5–10% overhead with 30–75% compression ratio. It reduces memory access with significant energy saving.

5.2.6 Global Buffer

Eyeriss accelerator employs Global Buffer (GLB) for data transfer between the external memory through an asynchronous interface. It also stores the fmaps, ifmaps, ofmaps, and psums for local computation. It preloads the next fmaps when the PEs are working on the current data. When the current computation is completed, it starts a new operation using next fmaps. The GLB can be configured differently to support RS dataflow with various layer dimensions.

5.2.7 Processing Element Architecture

Eyeriss Processing Element (PE) consists of three different types of spads to store – fmaps, ifmaps, and psums (Figure 5.29). They provide the enough memory bandwidth for data processing. The datapath is configured as three pipeline stages: spads access, fmaps, and ifmaps multiplication as well as psums accumulation. All the operations are done using 16 bits arithmetic. The multiplication results are truncated from 32 bits to 16 bits to reduce the memory storage. The psums are stored in spads and feed for accumulation. When the convolution is completed, it outputs the ofmaps.

The PE also supports the data gating to exploit the ineffectual zero. If the zero element is detected, the gating logic disables the filter spads read and datapath multiplication. It can reduce 45% of power dissipation.

5.2.8 Network-on-Chip (NoC)

Network-on-Chip (NoC) manages the data delivery between GLB and PE array. It is divided into Global Input Network (GIN) and Global Output Network (GON). GIN is targeted for data transfer between GLB and PEs using the single cycle

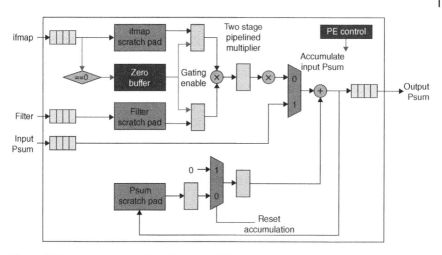

Figure 5.29 Eyeriss processing element architecture.

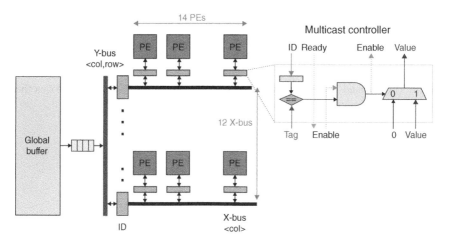

Figure 5.30 Eyeriss global input network.

multicast. It is implemented using two-level memory hierarchy with Y-bus and X-bus architecture (Figure 5.30).

The GLB transfers the data to the vertical Y-bus which links to 12 horizontal X-bus. Each X-bus connects to 14 PEs in the row (total 168 PEs). The top-level controller generates the packet with a unique tag <row, col> for data transfer. Twelve Multicast Controllers (MCs) on the Y-bus decode the tag-ID and compare the row tag against X-bus row-ID. Fourteen MCs on the X-bus check the col-tag with PE col-ID. It guarantees to deliver the packet to the correct PE. The unmatched X-bus and PEs are turned off to save power.

AlexNet with a different tag-ID is used as an example to illustrate the data delivery. It maps the logical array to physical processing elements (PEs) using replication and folding. AlexNet layers with CONV1, CONV2, CONV3, CONV4, and CONV5 are configured with row-ID (X-bus) and col-ID (PE) for ifmaps delivery. For tag-ID (0, 3), the highlighted X-bus and PEs are activated to receive the data during the convolution (Figures 5.31–5.34).

In order to map the neural network layers into the PE set, the mapping strategy is used to utilize the PE array for data sharing and partial sum accumulation with two exceptional cases:

- If the PE set is larger than the 168 physical PE array, the PE set is split into multiple strips to perform the convolution
- If the PE set is less than the 168 physical PE array with the width larger than 14 and height is larger than 12, Eyeriss can't support this configuration for processing

AlexNet is used to illustrate the PE mapping again. The 11×55 PE set of CONV1 is split into two segments 11×7 for processing. The 5×7 PE set of CONV2 is divided into two segments 5×14 and 5×13 and mapped into the PE array. The 3×13 PE set of CONV3, CONV4, and CONV5 are completely fitted into the PE array with three segments. With the RS dataflow, the PEs process multiple segmented data independently and recombine the result to complete the convolution. The unused PEs are disabled to save energy. It significantly improves the overall system performance (Figures 5.35–5.38).

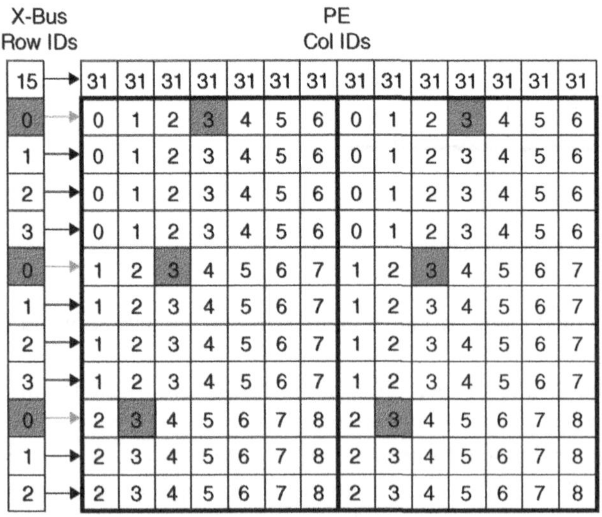

X-Bus Row IDs   **PE Col IDs**

Row														
15	31	31	31	31	31	31	31	31	31	31	31	31	31	31
0	0	1	2	3	4	5	6	0	1	2	3	4	5	6
1	0	1	2	3	4	5	6	0	1	2	3	4	5	6
2	0	1	2	3	4	5	6	0	1	2	3	4	5	6
3	0	1	2	3	4	5	6	0	1	2	3	4	5	6
0	1	2	3	4	5	6	7	1	2	3	4	5	6	7
1	1	2	3	4	5	6	7	1	2	3	4	5	6	7
2	1	2	3	4	5	6	7	1	2	3	4	5	6	7
3	1	2	3	4	5	6	7	1	2	3	4	5	6	7
0	2	3	4	5	6	7	8	2	3	4	5	6	7	8
1	2	3	4	5	6	7	8	2	3	4	5	6	7	8
2	2	3	4	5	6	7	8	2	3	4	5	6	7	8

Figure 5.31 Eyeriss processing element mapping (AlexNet CONV1).

X-Bus   PE
Row IDs   Col IDs

15 →	31	31	31	31	31	31	31	31	31	31	31	31	31	31
15 →	31	31	31	31	31	31	31	31	31	31	31	31	31	31
0 →	0	1	2	3	4	5	6	7	8	9	10	11	12	13
0 →	1	2	3	4	5	6	7	8	9	10	11	12	13	14
0 →	2	3	4	5	6	7	8	9	10	11	12	13	14	15
0 →	3	4	5	6	7	8	9	10	11	12	13	14	15	16
0 →	4	5	6	7	8	9	10	11	12	13	14	15	16	17
0 →	14	15	16	17	18	19	20	21	22	23	24	25	26	31
0 →	15	16	17	18	19	20	21	22	23	24	25	26	27	31
0 →	16	17	18	19	20	21	22	23	24	25	26	27	28	31
0 →	17	18	19	20	21	22	23	24	25	26	27	28	29	31
0 →	18	19	20	21	22	23	24	25	26	27	28	29	30	31

Figure 5.32   Eyeriss processing element mapping (AlexNet CONV2).

X-Bus   PE
Row IDs   Col IDs

0 →	0	1	2	3	4	5	6	7	8	9	10	11	12	31
0 →	1	2	3	4	5	6	7	8	9	10	11	12	13	31
0 →	2	3	4	5	6	7	8	9	10	11	12	13	14	31
0 →	0	1	2	3	4	5	6	7	8	9	10	11	12	31
0 →	1	2	3	4	5	6	7	8	9	10	11	12	13	31
0 →	2	3	4	5	6	7	8	9	10	11	12	13	14	31
0 →	0	1	2	3	4	5	6	7	8	9	10	11	12	31
0 →	1	2	3	4	5	6	7	8	9	10	11	12	13	31
0 →	2	3	4	5	6	7	8	9	10	11	12	13	14	31
0 →	0	1	2	3	4	5	6	7	8	9	10	11	12	31
0 →	1	2	3	4	5	6	7	8	9	10	11	12	13	31
0 →	2	3	4	5	6	7	8	9	10	11	12	13	14	31

Figure 5.33   Eyeriss processing element mapping (AlexNet CONV3).

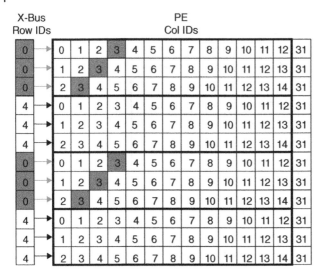

Figure 5.34 Eyeriss processing element mapping (AlexNet CONV4/CONV5).

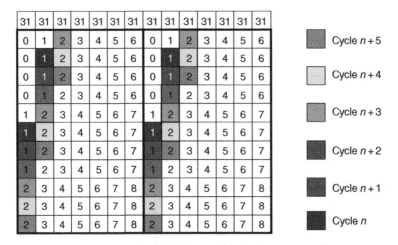

Figure 5.35 Eyeriss processing element operation (AlexNet CONV1).

5.2.9 Eyeriss v2 System Architecture

Recently, Eyeriss v2 accelerator [6–7] is developed to support irregular data pattern and network sparsity. Additional features are proposed as follows:

- A novel Network-on-Chip (NoC) hierarchical mesh supports high memory demands. When the data reuse is low, it transfers more data from the external network into PEs for processing. When the data reuse is high, it exploits the spatial data sharing to minimize the data movement.

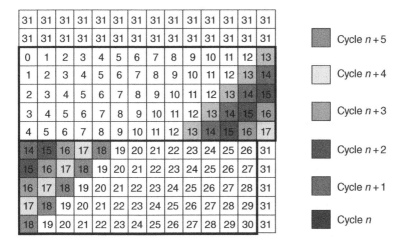

Figure 5.36 Eyeriss processing element operation (AlexNet CONV2).

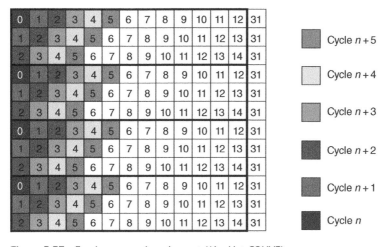

Figure 5.37 Eyeriss processing element (AlexNet CONV3).

- The Compressed Sparse Column (CSC) encoding scheme is adopted to eliminate the ineffectual zero operations. It reduces memory storage as well as data movement.
- Row Stationary Plus (RS+) dataflow is applied to fully utilize the PEs computational resource (Figures 5.39 and 5.40).

Eyeriss v1 accelerator adopts the two-level hierarchy strategy to connect the GLB and PEs through a flat multicast NoC for data processing. Eyeriss v2 accelerator uses hierarchical mesh configuration which groups the GLB and PEs into the cluster with flexible NoC. The separated NoC is employed to effectively transfer three

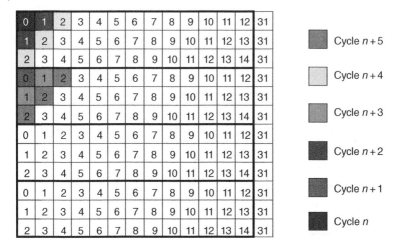

Cycle $n+5$

Cycle $n+4$

Cycle $n+3$

Cycle $n+2$

Cycle $n+1$

Cycle n

Figure 5.38 Eyeriss processing element operation (AlexNet CONV4/CONV5).

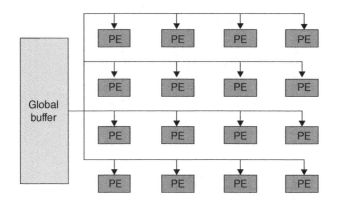

Eyeriss v1

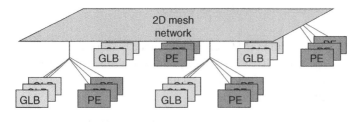

Eyeriss v2

Figure 5.39 Eyeriss architecture comparison.

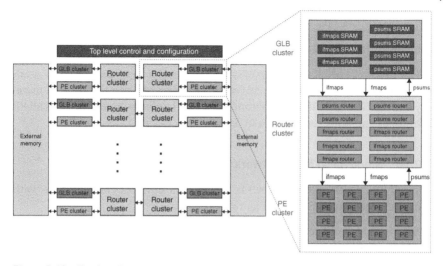

Figure 5.40 Eyeriss v2 system architecture.

Table 5.3 Eyeriss v2 architectural hierarchy.

Hierarchy	Number of components
Cluster array	8 × 2 PE clusters
	8 × 2 GLB clusters
	8 × 2 router clusters
GLB cluster	3 × ifmaps SRAM banks (1.5 kb)
	4 psums SRAM banks (1.875 kb)
Route cluster	3 × ifmaps routers (4 src/dst ports)
	3 × fmaps routers (2 src/dst ports)
	4 × psums routers (3 src/dst ports)
PE cluster	3 × 4 PEs

different types of data[3]: ifmap, fmaps, and psums. The hierarchical mesh is organized with cluster arrays: GLB Cluster, Router Cluster, and PE Cluster (Table 5.3).

The hierarchical mesh supports different data movements:

- ifmaps are loaded into the GLB cluster, they are either stored in the GLB memory or transferred to the router cluster

---

3 To be consistent between Eyeriss v1 and v2 architecture, it renames data types: iacts to ifmaps, weights to fmaps, and psum to psums from the paper.

- psums are stored in the GLB memory after computation, the final ofmaps are directly written back to the external memory
- fmaps are transferred to the router cluster and stored in PE spads for computation

The Eyeriss v2 accelerator supports two-level control logic like Eyeriss v1 accelerator. The top-level control directs the data transfer between the external memory and the GLB as well as the PEs and GLB. The low-level control handles all PE operations and processes the data in parallel.

5.2.10 Hierarchical Mesh Network

Typically, Network-on-Chip (NoC) is arranged in different configurations with the advantages and drawbacks (Figure 5.41):

- Broadcast network achieves high spatial data reuse with limited memory bandwidth. If the data reuse is low, it delivers the data to different destination sequentially resulting in performance degradation. The wider data bus improves the data delivery with the drawback of a larger buffer.
- The unicast network supports high memory bandwidth but not spatial data reuse resulting in high energy consumption.
- All-to-all network supports the high memory bandwidth and data reuse but not the network scaling resulting in high energy consumption.

The novel hierarchical mesh network (HM-NoC) is proposed to support RS+ dataflow. It is derived from the all-to-all network and reconfigured in four different modes:

- Broadcast: single input and single weight
- Unicast: multiple inputs and multiple weights

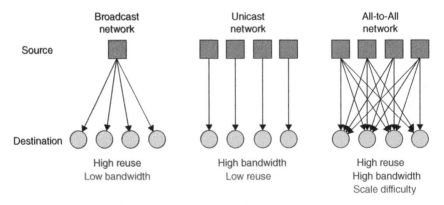

Figure 5.41 Network-on-Chip configurations.

- Grouped multicast: shared weights
- Interleaved multicast: shared inputs (Figure 5.42)

The HM-NoC consists of the source, destination, and router. They are grouped into the cluster during the design phase and fixed for the operation mode. The router cluster is connected to others through one-to-one, many-to-many, and source/destination connection (Figure 5.43).

The HM-NoC can be reconfigured as different neural network layers: convolutional layers, dept-wise convolutional layer, and fully connected layers.

- Convolutional layers: both ifmaps and fmaps are reused for the operations, they are configured as either grouped multicast or interleaved mode
- Depth-wise convolutional layer: only the fmaps can be reused, it broadcasts the fmaps to the PE and load the ifmaps from the GLB
- Fully connected layer: the ifmaps is broadcasted to every PE and the fmaps is loaded using the unicast mode

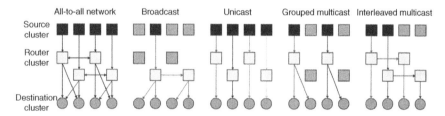

Figure 5.42 Mesh network configuration.

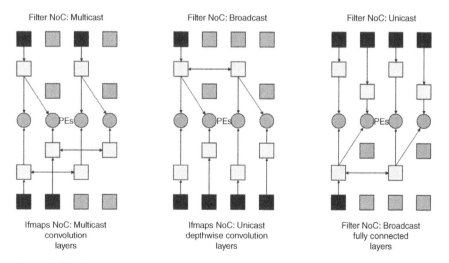

Figure 5.43 Eyeriss v2 hierarchical mesh network examples.

The router cluster has four source/destination ports to receive/transmit the data with different routing modes: broadcast, unicast, and grouped/interleaved multicast.

5.2.10.1 Input Activation HM-NoC

The three ifmaps router in the router cluster are connected to corresponding ifmaps SRAM banks in the GLB cluster. The ifmaps router uses three source/destination ports to receive and transmit the data among other clusters. The fourth source port loads the data from the memory and the fourth destination port transfers the data to the PE array (Figure 5.44).

5.2.10.2 Filter Weight HM-NoC

Each fmaps router in the router cluster is connected to each row of PE in the PE cluster. The vertical mesh connections are removed and the horizontal ones are kept for spatial reuse. The first source and destination ports are used to receive and transmit data between the neighbor clusters. The second source port loads the data from the external memory into the GLB and the second destination port connects to the row of PE within the cluster (Figure 5.45).

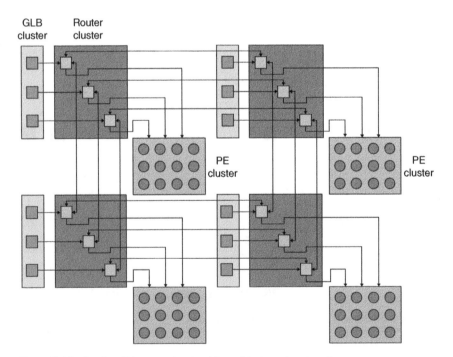

Figure 5.44 Eyeriss v2 input activation hierarchical mesh network.

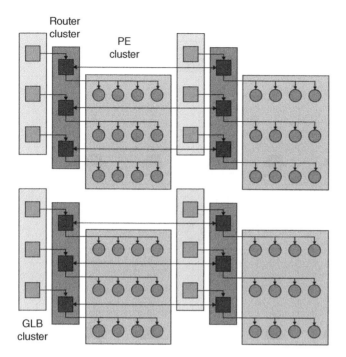

Figure 5.45 Weights hierarchical mesh network.

5.2.10.3 Partial Sum HM-NoC

The four psums routers in the router cluster connect to the psums SRAM bank in the GLB cluster and one column of PE in the PE cluster. The horizontal mesh connection is removed and the vertical one is used for psums accumulation. The first source port receives the data from the top cluster and the first destination port transfers the data to the bottom cluster. The second pair of source/destination ports are assigned for psums SRAM bank. The third source port is used for the top cluster PE column and the third destination port is connected to the bottom PE cluster column (Figure 5.46).

HM-NoC architecture offers strong scalability for Eyeriss v2 accelerator. To illustrate the performance improvement, it compares Eyeriss v1 and v2 accelerator performance using AlexNet, GoogleNet, and MobileNet with 256, 1024, and 16384 PEs. Eyeriss v1 accelerator shows minor performance improvement due to the insufficient memory bandwidth provided by multicast NoC design. The Eyeriss v2 accelerator performance is linearly proportional to the number of PEs. It achieves 85% improvement using 16384 PEs. In system performance session, it demonstrates how to further improve the performance with different configurations (Figures 5.47 and 5.48).

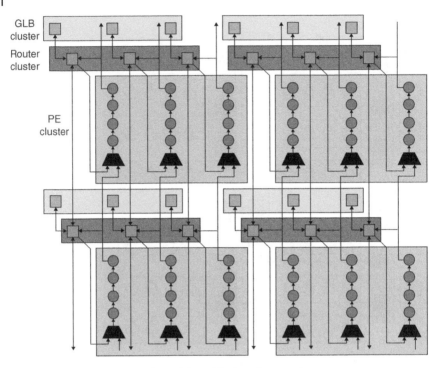

GLB cluster

Router cluster

PE cluster

Figure 5.46 Eyeriss v2 partial sum hierarchical mesh network.

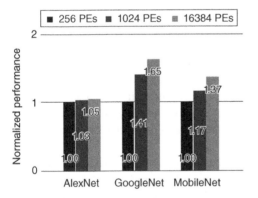

Figure 5.47 Eyeriss v1 neural network model performance. [6]

5.2.11 Compressed Sparse Column Format

For Eyeriss v2 accelerator, it applies the Compressed Sparse Column (CSC) encoding scheme to skip ineffectual zero operation for both ifmaps and fmaps to improve the system throughput and save energy (Figure 5.49). The CSC format is similar to

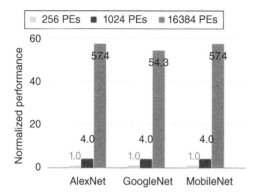

Figure 5.48 Eyeriss v2 neural network model performance. [6]

Filter weight matrix

Compressed sparse column format

Address index	1	2	3	4	5	6	6	7	8	9	10	
Data vector	A	B	C	D	E	F	G	H	I	J	K	L
Counter vector	1	0	0	0	1	2	3	1	1	0	0	0
Address vector	0	2	5	6	6	7	9	9	12			

Figure 5.49 Compressed sparse column format.

RLC one. It employs the data vector to store the nonzero elements. The counter vector records the number of leading zero from the previous nonzero element, the additional address vector indicates the starting address of the encoded segment. It allows the PE to easily process the nonzero data. The filter weight sparse matrix is used to illustrate the CSC encoding scheme. The PE reads the first column nonzero element A with starting address 0 and one leading 0. For the second column

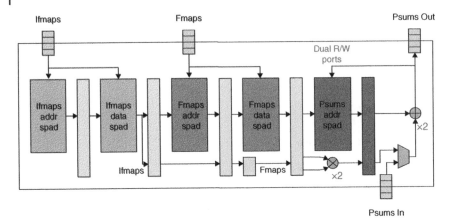

Figure 5.50 Eyeriss v2 PE architecture.

reading, it reads the nonzero element C with starting address 2^4 with none leading 0. For the fifth column reading, it repeats the starting address six to indicate the empty column before the element G. The last element shows the total number of the elements in the data vector (Figure 5.50).

Eyeriss v2 PE is modified to skip the ineffectual zero operations. It consists of seven pipeline stages with five spads to store the address/data of the ifmaps and fmaps as well as psums data. Due to data dependency, it first examines the address to determine the nonzero data. It also loads the ifmaps before fmaps to skip zero ifmaps operation. If the ifmaps are non-zero with corresponding non-zero fmaps, the data are pipelined for computation. For zero fmaps, it disables the pipeline to save energy.

The PE supports the Single Instruction Multiple Data (SIMD) operation. It fetches two fmaps into the pipeline for computation. It not only improves the throughput but reuses the ifmaps to enhance the system performance.

5.2.12 Row Stationary Plus (RS+) Dataflow

Eyeriss v2 accelerator enforces the data transfer to fully utilize the PEs with Row Stationary Plus (RS+) dataflow. The data is tiled and creates the spatial fragmentation to map the model dimension to a different PE dimension. For example, it resolves the depth-wise convolution issue for parallel processing idle PEs (Figure 5.51).

This approach has two advantages over its predecessor for performance improvement. It configures the system using the data pattern and supports different cluster size.

---

4 The starting address is corresponding to last data vector element B with address 2.

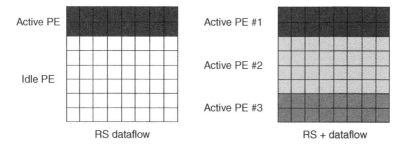

Figure 5.51 Eyeriss v2 row stationary plus dataflow.

Table 5.4 Eyeriss architecture.

	Eyeriss v1	Eyeriss v1.5	Eyeriss v2
Data precision	Activations and weights: 8 bits, Partial sums: 20 bits		
No. of PEs	192	192	192
No. of MACs	192	192	384
Network-on-Chip	Multicast	Hierarchical mesh	Hierarchical mesh
PE architecture	Dense	Dense	Sparse
PE SIMD support	No	No	Yes
Global buffer size	192 kb	192 kb	192 kb
Area (NAND2 gate)	1394 k	1394 k	2695 k

5.2.13 System Performance

To demonstrate the system performance, three Eyeriss architectures v1, v1.5, and v2 are implemented. Eyeriss v1.5 accelerator is similar to Eyeriss v2 design without the sparsity and SIMD supports but the area is reduced by half (Table 5.4).

For sparse AlexNet, Eyeriss v2 accelerator shows significant performance improvement 42.5× and energy efficiency 11.3×. The CSC encoding scheme reduces the ineffectual zero operations as well as the data traffic (Figures 5.52 and 5.53).

Due to the lack of data reuse in MobileNet, both Eyeriss v1.5 and v2 accelerators show minor performance improvement 10.9× and 12.6×. The CSC encoding approach is not effective for the depth-wise convolutional layer with single input and output channel (Figures 5.54 and 5.55).

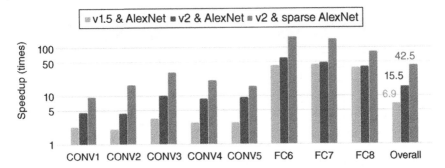

Figure 5.52 Eyeriss architecture AlexNet throughput speedup [6].

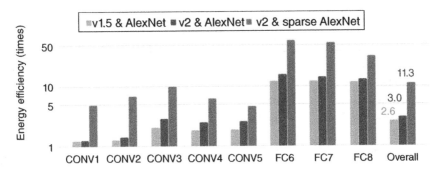

Figure 5.53 Eyeriss architecture AlexNet energy efficiency [6].

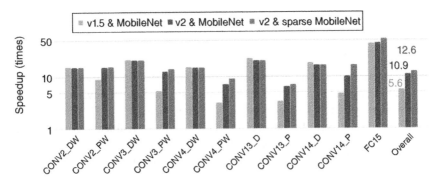

Figure 5.54 Eyeriss architecture MobileNet throughput speedup [6].

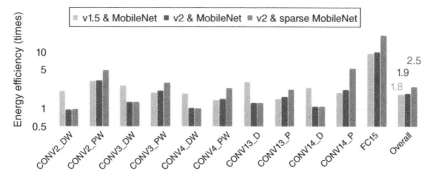

Figure 5.55 Eyeriss architecture MobileNet energy efficiency [6].

Exercise

1 What is efficiency loss if the DCNN filter size is changed to 5 × 5?

2 How do you modify the DCNN accelerator to support sparse encoding?

3 How do you transform Eyeriss 1D vector multiplication to 2D vector multiplication to support convolution?

4 What is the bottleneck of the Eyeriss v2 hierarchical mesh network?

5 What is the major difference between RLC and CSC encoding approaches?

6 Is the computation resource fully utilized with CSC format?

7 How do you further improve Eyeriss v2 performance?

References

1 Du, L., Du, Y., Li, Y. et al. (2018). A reconfigurable streaming deep convolutional neural network accelerator for internet of things. *IEEE Transactions on Circuits and Systems I* 65 (1): 198–208.

2 Du, L. and Du, Y. (2017). Machine learning - Advanced techniques and emerging applications. *Hardware Accelerator Design for Machine Learning*, Intecopen.com, pp. 1–14.

3 Han, S., Mao, H. and Dally, W.J. (2016). Deep compression: Compressing deep neural networks with pruning, trained quantization and huffman coding. *International Conference on Learning Representations (ICLR).*

4 Chen, Y.-H., Krishna, T., Emer, J., and Sze, V. (2017). Eyeriss: an energy-efficient reconfigurable accelerator for deep convolutional neural network. *IEEE Journal of Solid-State Circuits* 52 (1): 127–138.

5 Emer, J., Chen, Y-H., and Sze, V. (2019). *DNN Accelersator Architectures, International Symposium on Computer Architecture (ISCA 2019), Tutorial.*

6 Chen, Y.-H., Emer, J. and Sze, V. (2018). Eyeriss v2: A Flexible and High-Performance Accelerator for Emerging Deep Neural Networks. arXiv:1807.07928v1.

7 Chen, Y.-H., Yang. T.-J., Emer J., and Sze, V. (2019). Eyeriss v2: A Flexible Accelerator for Emerging Deep Neural Networks on Mobile Devices. arXiv: 1807.07928v2.

6

In-Memory Computation

To overcome the deep learning memory challenge, the in-memory computation [1–4] is proposed. It allows the logic and memory to stack together for high effective neural network processing. This chapter introduces several memory-centric Processor-in-Memory (PIM) architectures, Neurocube, Tetris, and NeuroStream accelerators.

6.1 Neurocube Architecture

Georgia Institute of Technologies Neurocube accelerator [5] integrates the parallel neural processing unit with the high-density 3D memory package Hybrid Memory Cube (HMC) to resolve the memory bottleneck. It supports data-driven programmable memory and exploits the algorithmic memory access pattern for computation through Memory-Centric Neural Computing (MCNC). Compared with the traditional instruction approach, the data is directly loaded from the stacked memory to the processing element (PE) for computation. It significantly reduces latency and speeds up the operation. Moreover, Programmable Neurosequence Generator (PNC) configures the system to support different neural network models.

6.1.1 Hybrid Memory Cube (HMC)

For High Bandwidth Memory (HBM), multiple memory dies are stacked together and connected to the high-performance processor through the interposer (Figure 6.1). Both the stacked memory dies and processor are designed separately. For HMC, the multiple memory dies are stacked on the top of the logic-based die and connected through TSV. The memory dies are divided into 16 vertical

Artificial Intelligence Hardware Design: Challenges and Solutions, First Edition.
Albert Chun Chen Liu and Oscar Ming Kin Law.
© 2021 The Institute of Electrical and Electronics Engineers, Inc. Published 2021
by John Wiley & Sons, Inc.

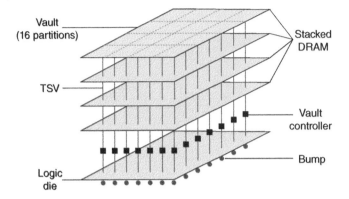

Figure 6.1 Neurocube architecture.

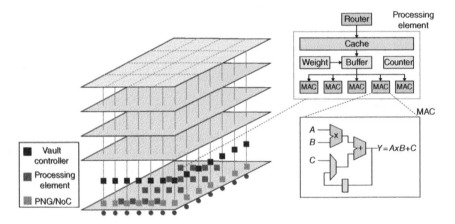

Figure 6.2 Neurocube organization.

partitions to form a vault with the vault controller. Each vault is connected to one processing element. All the vaults are operated independently to speed up the overall operations (Figure 6.2).

The Neurocube accelerator consists of the global controller, the Programmable Neurosequence Generator (PNC), the 2D mesh network, and the PEs. The Neurocube accelerator first maps the neural network model, the connection weight, and the states into the memory stack. The host initializes the command to PNC. It starts the state machine to stream the data from memory to the PE for computation. The data path between the memory stack and the logic layer is called priori.

The PE consists of eight Multiply-Accumulate (MAC) unit, the cache memory, a temporal buffer, and a memory module to store synaptic weight. PE performs the computation using modified 16 bits fixed-point format, 1 sign bit, 7 integer bits, and 8 fractional. It simplifies the hardware design with less error. Consider a neural network layer having eight neurons with three inputs from the previous layer. It can complete the computation within three cycles. On cycle 1, each MAC computes summation from first inputs, followed by second inputs with weights in cycle 2. All eight neurons are updated in cycle 3.

All PEs are connected using a 2D mesh network through a single router with six input and six output channels (four for neighbors and two for PE and memory). Each channel has 16 depth packet buffers. A rotating daisy chain priority scheme is used for packet distribution and the priority is updated every cycle. Each packet has operation identification (OP-ID) indicating the sequence order and an operation counter to control the packet sequence. An out-of-order packet is buffered in the SRAM cache. When all the inputs are available, they are moved to the temporal buffer for computation (Figure 6.3).

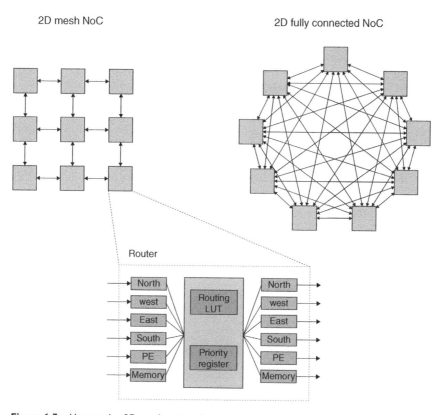

Figure 6.3 Neurocube 2D mesh network.

6.1.2 Memory Centric Neural Computing (MCNC)

Neurocube accelerator applies the MCNC approach for data-driven computation. For each layer neuron, the PNG generates the address for the connected neurons and their synaptic weights. It sends the address to Vault Controller (VC) and the VC returns the data back to PNG. The PNG encapsulates the data, the state, and output information into a packet with a specific MAC-ID. All the packets with corresponding neurons share the same MAC-ID. The packets are broadcasted to PEs through Network-on-Chip (NoC) router with the source ID (memory vault ID) and destination ID (PE ID) (Figure 6.4).

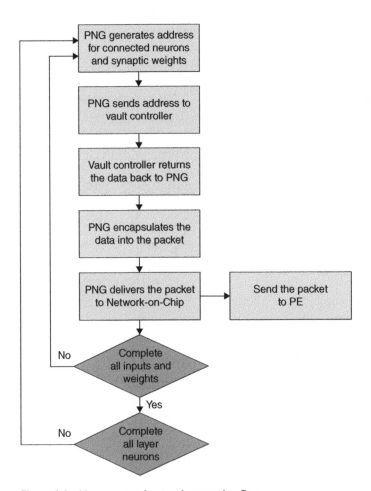

Figure 6.4 Memory-centric neural computing flow.

6.1.3 Programmable Neurosequence Generator (PNG)

PNG consists of address generator, configuration register, nonlinear activation function Look-Up Table (LUT) and the packet encapsulation/de-encapsulation logic. Each PNG is programmed by the global controller and the host sends the command to initialize the layer computation (Figure 6.5).

The PNG address generator is a programmable Finite State Machine (FSM) to create the address sequence for the neuron. It consists of three loops:

- A loop across all neurons in the layer
- A loop across all connections for a single neuron in the layer
- A loop across all MACs

The MAC unit calculates the state of one neuron at a time. This process is repeated until all the layer neurons are computed. The FSM controls three counters: the neuron counter, the connection counter, and the MAC counter (Figure 6.6).

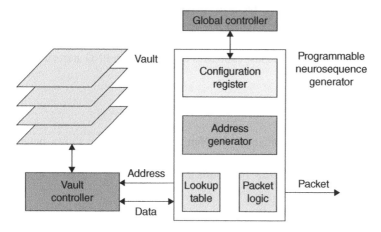

Figure 6.5 Programmable neurosequence generator architecture.

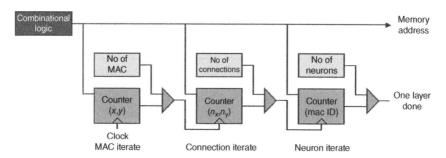

Figure 6.6 Neurocube programmable neurosequence generator.

To compute each connected neuron and synaptic weights address, it first receives the current state on the neuron counter (cur_x, cur_y) and the connectivity (n_x, n_y). The target address is calculated as

$$targ_x = cur_x + n_x \qquad\qquad (6.1)$$

$$targ_y = cur_y + n_y \qquad\qquad (6.2)$$

The physical memory address is computed

$$Addr = targ_x \times W + targ_y + Addr_{last} \qquad\qquad (6.3)$$

where
  W is the output image width
  $Addr_{last}$ is the previous layer last address

To program the PNG, the host sends the command to the configuration registers. It initializes the FSM to start the three loop operations, the MAC computation, the connection calculation, and the layer processing. When the neuron counter equals the total number of the layer neurons, the PNG has generated all the data address sequence for the layer. After the last address is computed, the PNG starts to program the next layer.

6.1.4 System Performance

Comparing the system performance, the Neurocube accelerator shows better energy efficiency than Nvidia GPU [6] Tegra K1 and GTX 780 with much less power dissipation. The architecture is suitable for embedded IoT inference operation (Table 6.1).

Table 6.1 Neurocube performance comparison.

Hardware	GPU		Neurocube	
Programmability	Yes	Yes	Yes	Yes
Hardware	Tegra K1	GTX 780	28 nm	15 nm
Bit precision	Floating	Floating	16 bits	16 bits
Throughput (GOPS/s)	76	1781	8	132.4
Power (W)	11	206.8	0.25	3.41
Efficiency (GOPS/s/W)	6.91	8.61	31.92	38.82
Number of input neurons	76 800		76 800	

6.2   Tetris Accelerator

Stanford University Tetris accelerator [7] adapts MIT Eyeriss Row Stationary (RS) dataflow with additional 3D memory – Hybrid Memory Cube (HMC) to optimize the memory access for in-memory computation.

6.2.1   Memory Hierarchy

For in-memory computation, the Tetris accelerator divides the HMC stack into sixteen 32 bits wide vaults. The vault connects with the logic-based die through high-speed TSV. Each stacked memory contains two banks per vault. The data is transferred from the memory array to the global sense amplifier to restore the signal magnitude. The data writes back to the stacked memory through the TSV data bus. Tetris accelerator replaces the crossbar switches with 2D mesh Network-on-Chip (NoC) to improve memory efficiency. It connects to the vault memory controller not only for local vault memory access but also remote vault through the NoC router. Neural Network (NN) engine is located in each vault. It consists of 2D processing elements (PE) array with 16 bits fixed-point ALU and 512 bits to 1024 bits register file. The global buffer is shared among all PEs for data reuse. Multiple NN engines can process single-layer neurons in parallel. With 3D memory, NN accumulator employs a large PE array (high performance) with a small buffer (less area) where the buffer-to-PE ratio is just half of Eyeriss one (Figures 6.7 and 6.8).

6.2.2   In-Memory Accumulation

Tetris accelerator implements in-memory accumulation to eliminate half of the ofmaps memory access and TSV data transfer (Figure 6.9). It resolves the memory bottleneck and improves overall performance. It combines back-to-back memory read/write access for better row buffer utilization.

For in-memory accumulation, it offers four different alternatives:

- Memory Controller Accumulation: The accumulators are placed at the logic die memory controller without stacked DRAM modification. This option can't eliminate any high-latency DRAM access and is not preferred for implementation.
- DRAM Die Accumulation: The accumulations are located close to the TSV driver. For 32 bits vault channels with 8× burst, two 16 bits adders are operated in SIMD mode and two 128 bits latches buffered the data during a burst. The address is sent to the bank. The accumulation logic performs the additions with updated value from the data bus. The results write back to the bank during write mode. The accumulation logic is placed outside the DRAM array which

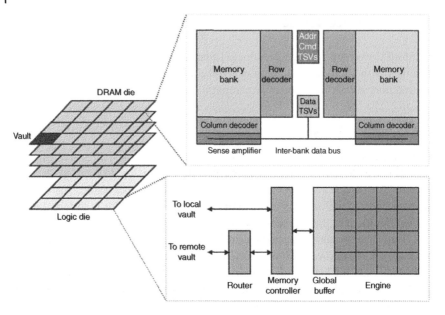

Figure 6.7 Tetris system architecture.

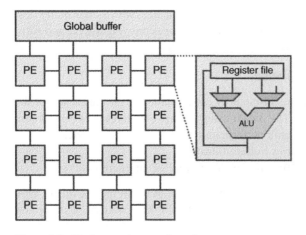

Figure 6.8 Tetris neural network engine.

doesn't affect array layout. This approach introduces slight latency overhead but is still small compared to DRAM access latency.

- Bank Accumulation: The accumulators are placed in DRAM bank. Two banks per vault can update the data in parallel without blocking the TSV bus. The accumulators are placed at the DRAM peripheral which doesn't affect array

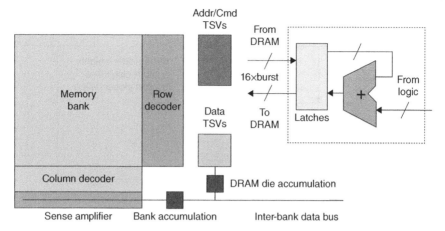

Figure 6.9 In-memory accumulation.

layout. The duplicate accumulator area is twice as the DRAM Die Accumulation area, but it is still small.

• Subarray Accumulation: The accumulators are located inside the DRAM bank with a shared bitline. This option can eliminate the data read out from the DRAM bank. The drawback is the large area overhead with DRAM array layout modification.

As a result, the DRAM die and bank accumulation options are chosen for the Tetris accelerator implementation.

6.2.3 Data Scheduling

For the dataflow sequencer, it applies MIT Row Stationary (RS) dataflow to map 2D convolution to 1D multiplication and fully utilizes the local resource for computation (Figure 6.10). It also maps a different size of convolution to a fixed size PE through folding and replication. To maximize the data reuse in global buffer, the bypass ordering is proposed with three options, Input Feature Maps/ Weights (IW) bypass (avoid the global buffer for ifmaps and fmaps), Output Feature Maps/Weights (OW) bypass (avoid the global buffer for ofmaps and fmaps) as well as Input/Output Feature Maps (IO) bypass (avoid the global buffer for ifmaps and ofmaps). For example, OW bypass splits the ifmaps into multiple chunks and fills the global buffer. Since ifmaps and ofmaps don't share the filters, the ofmaps is loaded into the register file directly. With RS dataflow, ifmaps locally convolves with fmaps in register file. Similarly, IO bypass uses the global buffer to store ifmaps and ofmaps. It offers a simple solution better than loop blocking and

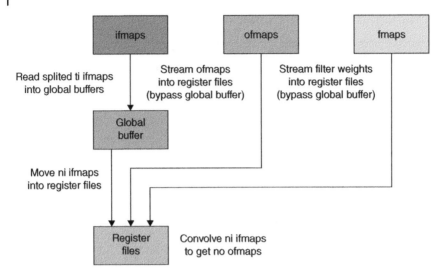

Figure 6.10 Global buffer bypass.

reordering scheme. Bypass ordering also benefits from in-memory accumulation that ofmaps update are directly pushed to memory to speed up the overall performance.

6.2.4 Neural Network Vaults Partition

To process a large neural network layer across the vault, different partition schemes are used (Figure 6.11):

- Batch Partitioning (Data-Parallelism) uses multiple accelerators to process multiple images in parallel to improve the overall throughput with the drawback of capacity and latency.
- Image Partitioning divides the large image into smaller tiles for processing. It fits for PE with better ifmaps/ofmaps locally but the fmaps needs to replicate across all vaults.
- Output Partitioning divides the ofmaps across the vaults. Since each ofmaps uses different fmaps, the fmaps can be fully separated for parallel operation. The ifmaps can be sent to all vaults for remote vault access.
- Input Partitioning distributes ifmaps across the vaults similar to output partitioning. Due to heavy read/write transfer of ofmaps using this scheme, the output partitioning is preferred over the input partitioning for implementation.

The hybrid partitioning scheme is proposed for the Tetris accelerator. The image partitioning is used for the first few convolutional layers to handle large image

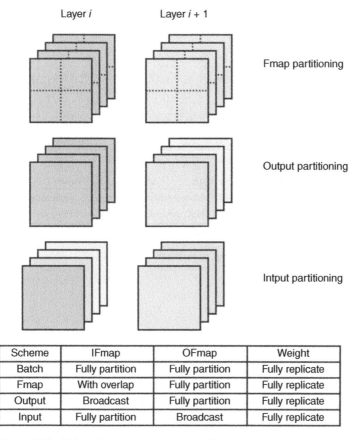

Figure 6.11 NN partitioning scheme comparison.

Scheme	IFmap	OFmap	Weight
Batch	Fully partition	Fully partition	Fully replicate
Fmap	With overlap	Fully partition	Fully replicate
Output	Broadcast	Fully partition	Fully replicate
Input	Fully partition	Broadcast	Fully replicate

when the filter weight reuse is not significant. For a fully connected layer, the output partitioning is used to handle large filter weight.

6.2.5 System Performance

To illustrate the system performance, the Tetris accelerator with 1 and 16 vaults (T1 and T16) compares with the system using 1 and 4 LPDDR3 memory channels (L1 and L4) as well as Neurocube accelerator with 16 vaults (N16) (Figure 6.12). The Tetris accelerator shows 37% performance improvement with 35–40% energy reduction over LPDDR3 L1 design. The performance is further improved by 12.9× with 9.2% higher energy with scaling design (T16). The Tetris accelerator (T16) shows 4.1× performance over LPDDR3 L4 design with 1.48× less energy.

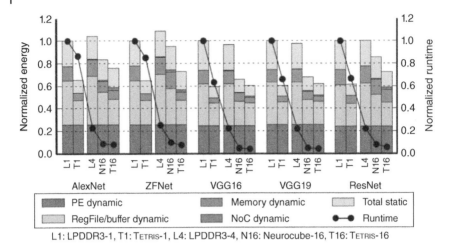

L1: LPDDR3-1, T1: TETRIS-1, L4: LPDDR3-4, N16: Neurocube-16, T16: TETRIS-16

Figure 6.12 Tetris performance and power comparison [7].

6.3 NeuroStream Accelerator

6.3.1 System Architecture

University of Bologna NeuroStream accelerator [8] is derived from Processor-in-Memory (PIM) architecture. It consists of four Smart Memory Cubes (SMCs) which are the modular extension of the standard Hybrid Memory Cube (HMC) (Figure 6.13). All the SMCs are connected through the mesh network. Each SMC hosts a NeuroCluster with 16 clusters on its Logic-Base (LoB) die. Each cluster supports four RSIC-V Processing Elements (PEs) and eight NeuroStream (NST) coprocessors. Every PE is equipped with Memory Management Unit (MMU) and the Translation Look-aside Buffer (TLB) to translate the address between the host and the NeuroCluster. Each cluster supports the Direct Memory Access (DMA) engine for data transfer between the DRAM vaults and the internal ScratchPad Memory (SPM). There is total 1 Gb DRAM in four stacked DRAM dies and 32 vaults with 32 Mb memory storage. The key features of the NeuroStream accelerator are listed as follows:

- NeuroCluster frequency: 1 GHz
- NeuroStream per cluster: 8
- RISC-V cores per cluster: 4
- Instruction cache per core: 1 kb
- Scratchpad per cluster: 128 kb

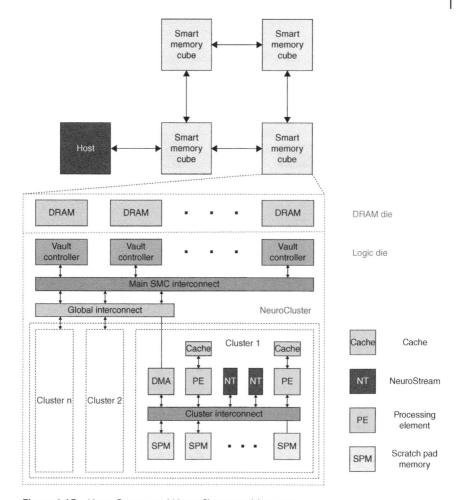

Figure 6.13 NeuroStream and NeuroCluster architecture.

- Scratchpad interleaving: Word-Level-Interleaved
- Scratchpad banking factor: 2
- Cluster per SMC: 16

Each RSIC-V processor has four pipeline stages for in-order execution as well as 1 kb private instruction cache. The internal SPM is based on multiple bank Word-Level-Interleaved (WLT) using cluster interconnect to provide low latency connectivity.

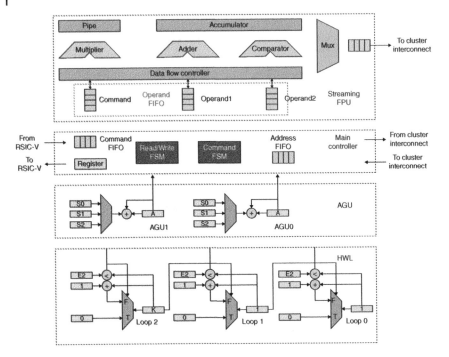

Figure 6.14 NeuroStream coprocessor architecture.

6.3.2 NeuroStream Coprocessor

NeuroStream (NST) coprocessor consists of the main controller, three Hardware-Loops (HWLs), two Address Generation Units (AGUs), and the 32 bits floating point datapath. The controller receives the command from the processor through cluster interconnect and issues a maximum of two transactions per cycle for the Multiply-Accumulate (MAC) unit. It also employs FIFO to keep the Floating-Point Unit (FPU) busy and hide the programming latency. It applies the memory-mapped control interface to communicate with other processors. Each HWL is a programmable FSM that handles the nested loop for the convolution. The AGU is programmed to generate a complex stride SPM access pattern. The NST coprocessor supports convolution, max-pooling, activation operation, and some basic back-propagation functions. It also performs the basic computation, dot product, matrix multiplication, linear transformation, and weighted sum/average (Figure 6.14).

6.3.3 4D Tiling Mechanism

4D Tile is a subset of the input volume (input tile) and output volume (output tile) of the convolutional layer (l) with ($T_{Xi}^{(l)}$, $T_{Yi}^{(l)}$, $T_{Ci}^{(l)}$, $T_{Co}^{(l)}$) tuple where $T_{Xi}^{(l)}$ and $T_{Yi}^{(l)}$ are the input tile width and height, $T_{Ci}^{(l)}$ and $T_{Co}^{(l)}$ are the number of tile input and output channels. The output dimensions of each tile are determined by the input width/height, the filter dimensions, striding, and zero-padding parameters. 4D Tile applies the row-major data layout approach and changes 2D input volume into 1D vector. It allows DMA to transfer the entire tile to the processing cluster through a single data request (Figure 6.15).

4D Tile also accounts for the sliding filter window using the overlapping approach. It stores both the raw tiles and augmented tiles (overlapped region) in a row-major data format which avoids the high-speed memory data fragmentation issue. It fetches the complete tile (raw and augmented tiles) from DRAM using a single data request and converts part of the raw tiles into augmented one for the next layer during DRAM writeback.

To compute the output tile, the partial sum is reused. After all the input tiles are read, the activation and pooling are completed, the partial sum Q (also output tile) writes back to DRAM once

$$Q = Q + X \times K_Q \tag{6.4}$$

where

Q is the partial sum
X is the input tile with $X = M, N, P \ldots$
K is the filter weight

To convert the augmented tile for the next layer $(l+1)$, the tile has four regions (raw, A, B, C), the raw region of $T_0^{(l+1)}$ is written back to DRAM, followed by A, B, and C regions of $T_0^{(l+1)}$ after $T_1^{(l)}, T_3^{(l)}, T_4^{(l)}$ are computed.

Since there is no data overlap among the augmented tiles, each cluster can execute one tile at a time to reduce the data transfer. All the tile information is stored in the list. The PE processes every tile based on the list order. Each cluster applies the ping-pong strategy to minimize the setup time and latency impact. When the tile is computed inside the cluster, another tile is fetched from memory. It repeats the process until all the tiles in the layer are computed. All the clusters are synchronized before processing the next layer.

Inside the cluster, each master PE partitions the tile in the order of $T_{Xo}^{(l)}$, $T_{Yo}^{(l)}$, and $T_{Co}^{(l)}$ dimensions to avoid synchronization. $T_{Ci}^{(l)}$ is used for additional partitions for arbitrarily sized tile and corner tile. 4D Tile performs the spatial and temporal computation assignment inside the cluster.

6.3.4 System Performance

The roofline plot is used to illustrate NeuroStream processor performance. The left axis shows the performance and the right one is the memory bandwidth. The bottom axis indicates the operating intensity. The plot highlights the importance of the tile size toward different neural network model performance. It is not effective for ResNet with 1×1 network due to the tile initialization penalty (Figure 6.16).

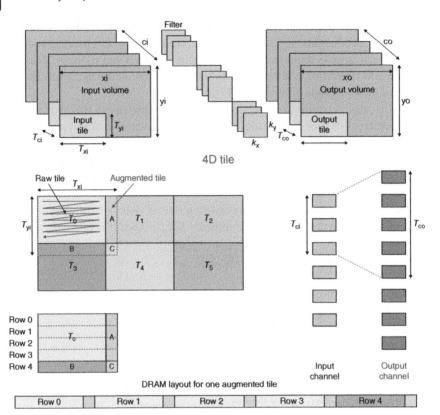

Figure 6.15 NeuroStream 4D tiling.

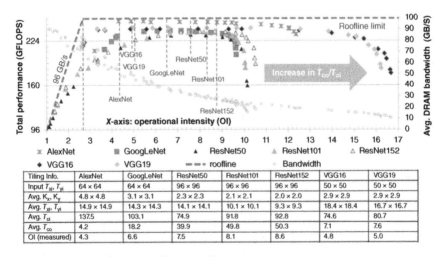

Tiling Info.	AlexNet	GoogLeNet	ResNet50	ResNet101	ResNet152	VGG16	VGG19
Input T_{xi}, T_{yi}	64 × 64	64 × 64	96 × 96	96 × 96	96 × 96	50 × 50	50 × 50
Avg. K_x, K_y	4.8 × 4.8	3.1 × 3.1	2.3 × 2.3	2.1 × 2.1	2.0 × 2.0	2.9 × 2.9	2.9 × 2.9
Avg. T_{xi}, T_{yi}	14.9 × 14.9	14.3 × 14.3	14.1 × 14.1	10.1 × 10.1	9.3 × 9.3	18.4 × 18.4	16.7 × 16.7
Avg. T_{ci}	137.5	103.1	74.9	91.8	92.8	74.6	80.7
Avg. T_{co}	4.2	18.2	39.9	49.8	50.3	7.1	7.6
OI (measured)	4.3	6.6	7.5	8.1	8.6	4.8	5.0

Figure 6.16 NeuroStream roofline plot [8].

Exercise

1 What is the Hybrid Memory Cube Technology?

2 What are Hybrid Memory Cube limitations for Deep Learning Application?

3 How do you improve Neurocube 2D mesh network design?

4 How do you enhance Tetris in-memory accumulation for data reuse?

5 How do you improve Tetris parallel partitioning scheme for parallel processing?

6 What is the major difference between Hybrid Memory Cube (HMC) and Smart Memory Cube (SMC)?

7 Can you modify NeuroStream 4D tiling scheme to support network sparsity?

References

1 Singh, G., Chelini, L., Corda, S., et al. (2019). Near-Memory Computating: Past, Present and Future. arXiv:1908.02640v1.

2 Azarkhish, E., Rossi, D., Loi, I., and Benini, L. (2016). Design and evaluation of a processing-in-memory architecture for the smart memory cube. In: *Architecture of Computing Systems – ARCS 2016*, 19–31. Springer.

3 Azarkhish, E., Pfister, C., Rossi, D. et al. (2017). Logic-Base interconnect design for near memory computing in the smart memory cube. *IEEE Transactions on Very Large Scale Integration (VLSI) Systems* 25 (1): 210–223.

4 Jeddeloh, J. and Keeth, B. (2012). Hybrid memory cube new dram architecture increases density and performance. *2012 Symposium on VLSI Technology (VLSIT)*, 87–88.

5 Kim, D., Kung, J., Chai, S., et al. (2016). Neurocube: a programmable digital neuromorphic architecture with high-density 3D memory. *2016 ACM/ IEEE 43rd Annual International Symposium on Computer Architecture (ISCA)*, 380–392.

6 Cavigelli, L., Magno, M., and Benini, L. (2015). Accelerating real-time embedded scene labeling with convolutional networks. *2015 52nd ACM/EDAC/IEEE Design Automation Conference (DAC)*, 1–6.

7 Gao, M., Yang, X., Horowitz, M., and Kozyrakis, C. (2017). Tetris: scalable and efficient neural network acceleration with 3D memory. *Proceedings of the Twenty-second International Conference on Architectural Support for Programming Languages and Operating Systems,* 751–764.

8 Azarkhish, E., Rossi, D., Loi, I., and Benini, L. (2018). Neurostream: scalable and energy efficient deep learning with smart memory cubes. *IEEE Transactions on Parallel and Distributed Systems* 29(2): 420–434.

7

Near-Memory Architecture

7.1 DaDianNao Supercomputer

The Institute of Computing Technology (ICT), Chinese Academy of Science, DaDianNao supercomputer [1] is proposed to resolve DianNao accelerator [2] memory bottleneck through massive eDRAM. Neural Functional Unit (NFU) provides large storage to accommodate all the synapse to avoid the data transfer between external memory. The tile-based design is adopted to spread out the NFUs in 16 tiles at the four corners. All the NFUs are time-interleaved with four eDRAM banks to compensate for the eDRAM high latency, destructive read, and periodic refresh. The NFU can process 16 input neurons of 16 output neurons (total 256 neurons) in parallel to speed up the operation (Figure 7.1).

7.1.1 Memory Configuration

All the tiles are connected through the fat-tree [3]. It reads the input neuron from the central eDRAM to initialize the computation and writes back the output neurons into central eDRAM after operations. All the intermediate values are stored in local eDRAM to avoid transfer between NFU and central eDRAM. The central eDRAM is further divided into two banks, one for input neurons and the other for output neurons. For HyperTransport (HT), interfaces (East, South, West, and North) are used for high-speed communication. The DaDianNao supercomputer is connected through 2D mesh network using Hyper Transport (HT) interface with East, South, West, and North links. Each HT supports 16 pairs' bidirectional differential links run at 1.6 GHz and provides the memory bandwidth of 6.4 Gb/s in either direction.

Artificial Intelligence Hardware Design: Challenges and Solutions, First Edition.
Albert Chun Chen Liu and Oscar Ming Kin Law.
© 2021 The Institute of Electrical and Electronics Engineers, Inc. Published 2021
by John Wiley & Sons, Inc.

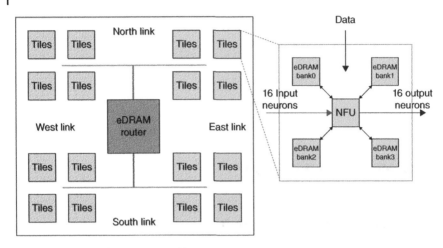

Figure 7.1 DaDianNao system architecture.

The wormhole router is implemented to support high-speed data transfer with five input/output ports (four directions and injection/ejection ports). The router is operated at four pipeline stages: Routing Computation (RC), Virtual Channel Allocation (VA), Switch Allocation (SA), and Switch Traversal (ST).

7.1.2 Neural Functional Unit (NFU)

NFU consists of multiple computational blocks, adder block, multiplier block, max block, and transfer blocks (Figure 7.2).

- Adder block is configured either as 256 inputs, 16 outputs adder tree, or 256 parallel adders
- Multiplier block is arranged as 256 parallel multipliers
- Max block performs 16 parallel max operations
- Transfer block consists of two independent sub-blocks performing 16 piecewise linear interpolations

The NFU can be arranged in pipeline configurations to support different operations: convolutions (FP and BP),[1] the classifier (FP and BP), the pooling (FP and BP), and Local Response Normalization (LRN) (Figure 7.3).

Each computational block supports the basic 16 bits operations, two or more blocks combine to perform 32 bits operation. For example, two 16 bits adders form 32 bits adders and four 16 bits multipliers construct 32 bits multipliers. The 16 bits

---

1 Forward Propagation (FP) and Backward Propagation (BP).

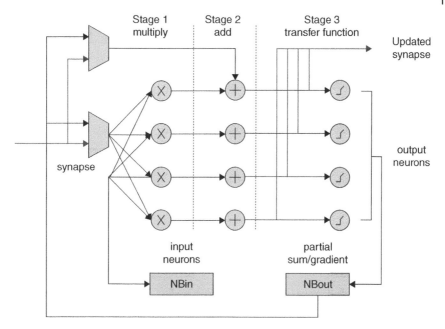

Figure 7.2 DaDianNao neural functional unit architecture.

operations are good enough for inference but reduce the training accuracy. Therefore, 32 bits fixed-point operations are used for training with an error rate of less than 1%.

The DaDianNao supercomputer is programmed with the sequence of simple node instructions to control the tile operations with three operands: start address (read/write), step (stride), and the number of iterations. NFU runs as two modes, the row operating processes one row at a time and the batch learning processes multiple rows in parallel. It benefits the synapse reuse with slower convergence.

DaDianNao supercomputer is operated with multiple node mapping. The input neurons are first distributed to all node tiles through the fat-tree network. It performs the convolution and pooling locally with low internode communication except for the boundary input neurons for mapping. The local response normalization is computed internally without any external communication. Finally, all the results are grouped for classification with high data traffic. At the end of every layer operations, the output neurons write back to central eDRAM and become the input neurons for the next layer. All the operations are done using computing-and-forward communication scheme, each node computes the input neurons locally and sends out the results for the next operations without the global synchronization (Figure 7.4).

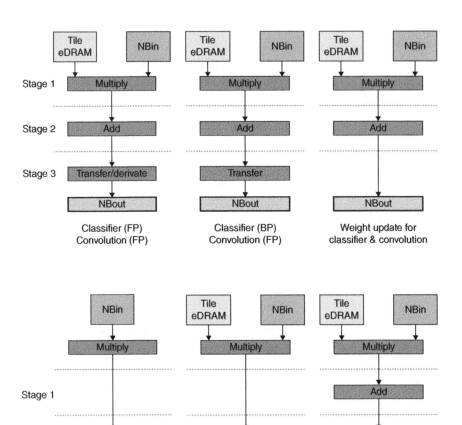

Figure 7.3 DaDianNao pipeline configuration.

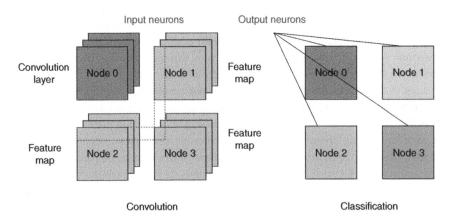

Figure 7.4 DaDianNao multi-node mapping.

7.1.3 System Performance

The DaDianNao supercomputer performance is compared with NVIDIA K20M GPU based on layer-by-layer operations. Due to different layer memory requirement, the comparisons are done using 1, 4, 16, and 64 node configurations. With DaDianNao supercomputer, the performance is improved by 21.38 × (1 node), 79.81 × (2 nodes), 216.72 × (4 nodes), and 450.65 × (64 nodes) due to large operations supported by each node. Moreover, the energy improvement is about 330.56 × (1 node), 323.74 × (2 nodes), 276.04 × (4 nodes), and 150.31 × (16 nodes) over NVIDIA GPU (Figures 7.5–7.8).

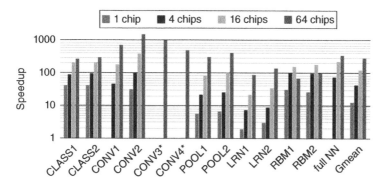

Figure 7.5 DaDianNao timing performance (Training) [1].

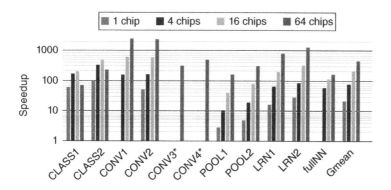

Figure 7.6 DaDianNao timing performance (Inference) [1].

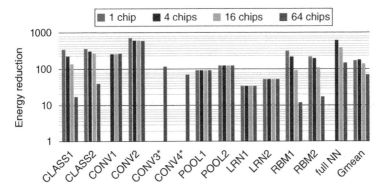

Figure 7.7 DaDianNao power reduction (Training) [1].

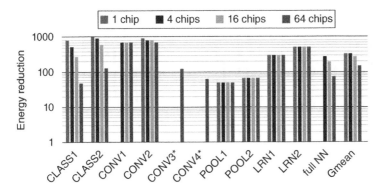

Figure 7.8 DaDianNao power reduction (Inference) [1].

7.2 Cnvlutin Accelerator

University of Toronto Cnvlutin[2] accelerator [4] is derived from DaDianNao architecture. It applies the massively parallel multiplication lanes to speed up the operations. Multiple DaDianNao accelerators are connected through a high-speed interface for large neural network processing. However, DaDianNao accelerator can't eliminate the ineffectual zero operations. It degrades overall performance with higher power dissipation.

For convolutional operation, the features are extracted from the input neurons. The negative value indicates the features do not exist. The ReLU layer rectifies the output resulting in network sparsity. It accounts for 40% of the total elements.

---

2 Cnvlutin is derived from convolution without "O".

Cnvlutin accelerator is proposed to resolve the network sparsity with new memory architecture. It decouples the original parallel multiplication lanes into independent groups and encodes the nonzero elements in new data format during the operation. The new data format allows the multiplication lanes to skip over the ineffectual zero operations and process all the data in parallel. It significantly improves overall performance with less power.

7.2.1 Basic Operation

To illustrate the DaDianNao basic operation, the input neurons are loaded from the input Neuron Buffer (NBin) into the neuron lane and the filter weights are fed from the Synapse Buffer (SB) lane into the synapse sublane. For every cycle, each neuron lane broadcasts its neuron to the corresponding synapse sublane for dot product multiplication. The adders combine the dot product results to generate the partial sums stored in the Output Neuron Buffer (NBout) for future accumulation. This approach couples all the input neuron lanes with the synapse sublane to perform parallel multiplication within three clock cycles. However, it can't eliminate four ineffectual zero operations during the computation (Figure 7.9).

Cnvlutin accelerator is modified to eliminate the ineffectual zero operations. It first divides the DaDianNao architecture into the front-end and back-end units. The front-end unit consists of the neuron lanes, synapse sublanes, and multiplier. The back-end unit consists of the adder tree and NBout. The front-end unit is further split into two filter groups. Each group contains one neuron lane and a filter synapse sublane. For every cycle, each group performs two dot products' multiplication and feeds the results into the adder to generate the partial sum for the output neuron lane (Figure 7.10).

The neuron lanes decouple with others and skip the ineffectual zero using the Zero-Free Neuron Array format (ZFNAf). It stores the nonzero neuron and its offset are stored in (value, offset). For example, the original stream of neurons $(1, 0, 3)$ and $(0, 2, 4)$ can be encoded as $((1, 0), (3, 2))$ and $((2, 1), (4, 2))$, respectively. During cycle 0, the neuron value 1 and its offset 0 are loaded into the neuron lanes. Then it multiplies with the corresponding synapse lanes 1 and -1. The results are fed into the adder to generate the partial sum for accumulation. Similarly, it performs the multiplication with the neuron value 2 and its offset 1 simultaneously. The convolution is completed within two cycles using the decoupled neuron lanes and new ZFNAf data format. It significantly speeds up the operation and saves the power.

7.2.2 System Architecture

DaDianNao accelerator consists of 16 NFU which has 16 neuron lanes and 16 filter lanes with 16 synapse lanes (total 256) to produce 16 partial sums for 16 output neurons. Each NFU has 256 multipliers for dot product multiplication,

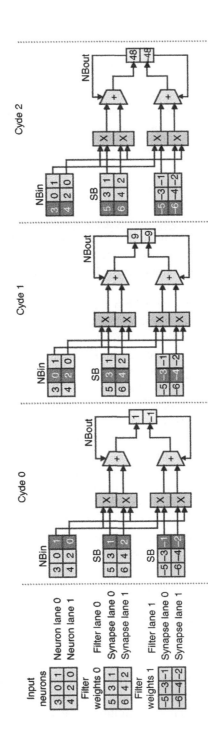

Figure 7.9 DaDianNao basic operation.

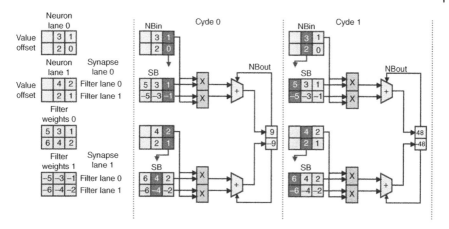

Figure 7.10 Cnvlutin basic operation.

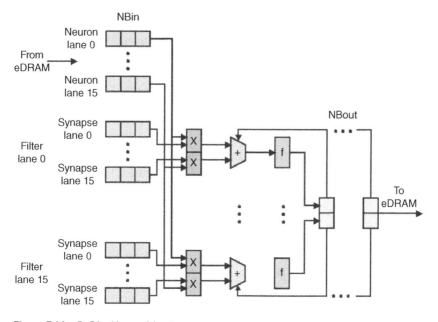

Figure 7.11 DaDianNao architecture.

16 adders for partial sum addition, and an additional adder for output neuron calculation. The number of neuron lanes and filter per unit can be changed dynamically during operation (Figure 7.11).

Cnvlutin accelerator partitions the neuron lanes and the synapse lanes into 16 independent groups. Each group contains a single neuron lane and 16 synapse

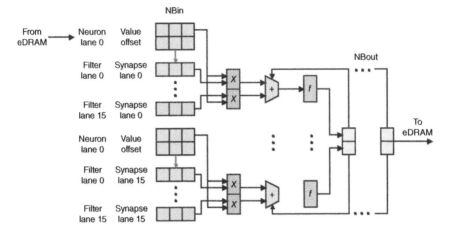

Figure 7.12 Cnvlutin architecture.

lanes from different filters. For every cycle, each synapse lane fetches the single neuron pair (neuron, offset) from NBin and performs the multiplication with the corresponding synapse entry based on its offset. The partial sums are accumulated using 16 adders. It keeps the NFUs busy all the time and the overall performance is dramatically improved with less power dissipation (Figure 7.12).

7.2.3 Processing Order

Cnvlutin accelerator applies the brick assignment rather than DaDianNao inter-leaved approach to improve the pipeline efficiency (Figure 7.13). For interleaved approach,[3] a block of 16 input neurons is loaded into 16 neuron lanes NL_0 to NL_{15} with labels n (0, 0, 0) to n (0, 0, 15) where (x, y, z) specifies the Neural Memory (NM) array location. The 256 filter weights are partitioned into 16 synapse lanes in 16 filter lanes. For example, SL_0^0 to SL_{15}^0 are referred to the 16 synapse lanes in unit 0 with the filter weights $s^0(0, 0, 0)$ to $s^0(0, 0, 15)$ from NM array. Then, the input neuron in the neuron lanes NL_0 to NL_{15} multiplies with the corresponding synapse from SL_0^0 to SL_{15}^0 in unit 0 to SL_0^{15} to SL_{15}^{15} in unit 15. This approach can perform massive multiplications in parallel but can't handle the ineffectual zero operations (Figure 7.14).

For the brick assignment, the Cnvlutin accelerator divides the window entry into 16 slices, one per neuron. The filter weights are partitioned into synapse lanes similar to the order of the DaDianNao accelerator. For every cycle, one neuron per slice is fetched into the group of the 16 neuron lanes for operation. Let n' (x, y, z) be the input neuron with (value, offset) stored at NM array location (x, y, z), the

---

3 Both interleaved and brick assignment are redrawn to clarify the processing order.

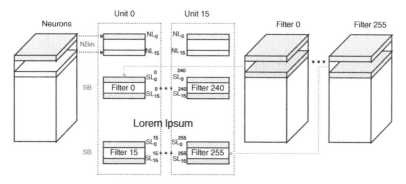

Figure 7.13 DaDianNao processing order.

input neuron n' $(0, 0, 0)$ to n' $(0, 0, 15)$ is first fetched to neuron lanes NL_0 to NL_{15}. It performs the multiplication with corresponding synapse lanes SL_0^0 to SL_0^{15} in unit 0 to SL_{15}^{240} to SL_{15}^{255} in unit 15. If brick 0 has only one nonzero value, then the next nonzero value n' $(1, 0, 0)$ is fetched into unit 0 rather than n' $(0, 0, 1)$. It keeps all the units busy all the time.

Since the input neurons assignment order is changed, the order of the synapse stored in the synapse sublane is also altered. For example, $S^0 (0, 0, 0)$ to $S^{15} (0, 0, 0)$ are stored in the first slice SL_0^0 to SL_{15}^0 for unit 0 NL_0 and $S^{240} (0, 0, 15)$ to $S^{255} (0, 0, 15)$ are stored in the last slice SL_{15}^{240} to SL_{15}^{255} for unit 15 NL_{15}.

7.2.4 Zero-Free Neuron Array Format (ZFNAf)

Zero-Free Neuron Array format (ZFNAf) is proposed to support the zero skipping similar to Compressed Sparse Row (CSR) format. ZFNAf stores the nonzero neurons with offset as (value, offset) pair without memory storage saving. It groups the nonzero neuron together (called brick) corresponding to the same fetch blocks and aligned with the input neuron dimension at the same HM array location (x, y). It uses the first neuron coordinate in brick to index the neuron array. It reduces the overhead and keeps the offset short (Figure 7.15).

To encode the neuron, the Input Buffer (IB) first reads the 16 neuron entries from NBout and increments its offset counter. It transfers the nonzero data into the Output Buffer (OB) using Offset Count (OC) index. If all 16 neuron entries are processed, the results are stored in the Neural Memory (NM).

7.2.5 The Dispatcher

Cnvlutin accelerator employs a dispatcher to keep the neuron lanes busy all the time. It divides the NM into 16 independent banks and the input neuron slices are distributed over the bank. It uses a Brick Buffer (BB) to connect to NM bank through a 16 neuron wide bus. It reads one brick from each bank and broadcasts the nonzero

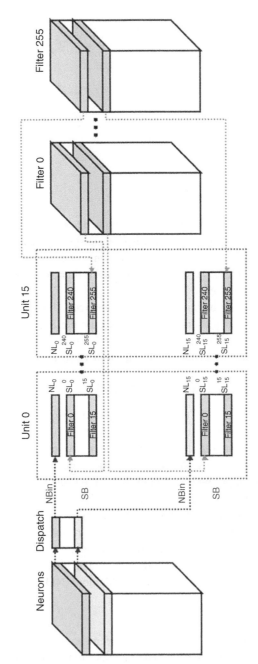

Figure 7.14 Cnvlutin processing order.

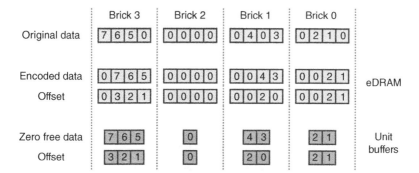

Figure 7.15 Cnvlutin zero free neuron array format.

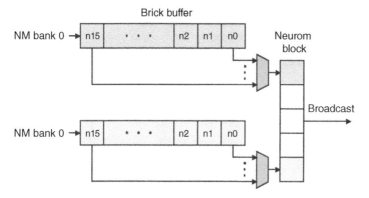

Figure 7.16 Cnvlutin dispatch.

neuron to the corresponding neuron lane for processing. It keeps on fetching the brick to avoid the NM stalling and improve overall throughput (Figure 7.16).

7.2.6 Network Pruning

Cnvlutin accelerator allows dynamic neuron pruning. It sets the neuron to zero when it is below the layer threshold. Then it skips the inefficient neuron and synapse operations. The threshold is calculated through a gradient descent approach.

7.2.7 System Performance

Compared with the DaDianNao supercomputer, the performance is improved by 37%. It is further enhanced through network pruning (Figure 7.17). The NM power is higher with a 2% overhead for additional logic processing. However, the overall power is still 7% lower than the DaDianNao supercomputer (Figure 7.18).

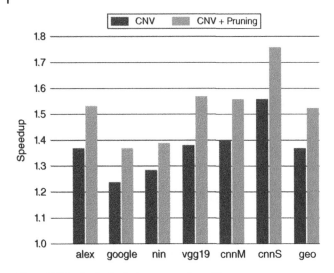

Figure 7.17 Cnvlutin timing comparison [4].

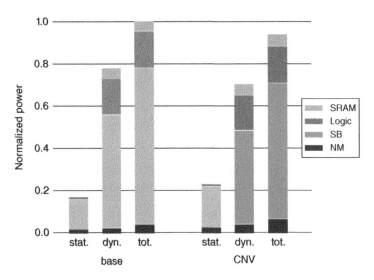

Figure 7.18 Cnvlutin power comparison [4].

7.2.8 Raw or Encoded Format (RoE)

Since the ineffectual element may not be fully encoded, Cnvlutin[2] accelerator [5] proposes a Raw or Encoded Format (RoE) to solve this problem. RoE uses first bit as encode flag to identify if the brick is encoded or not with four 16 bits fixed point value (total 65 bits). The encode format is <encode flag, <offset, value> <offset,

value> <offset, value> <offset, value>>. For example, (2, 1, 3, 4) can't fit within 65 bits. It is stored in raw format <0, 2, 1, 3, 4>, where 0 indicates the data is raw followed by four 16 bits number. The value (1, 2, 0, 4) can be encoded using RoE <1 <0, 1> <1, 2><3, 4>> where $1 + (16 + 4) \times 3 = 61$ bits. It significantly reduces the memory overhead.

7.2.9 Vector Ineffectual Activation Identifier Format (VIAI)

Vector Ineffectual Activation Identifier Format (VIAI) uses extra bits vector I to encode the nonzero offset. If a brick contains (1, 2, 0, 4), the 4 bits element I vector is encoded as (1, 1, 0, 1). For four bricks of 16 activations, it introduces 16/256 (or 6.25%) area penalty. The format is compressed to store the effectual valve. The previous example is compressed as (1101, 1, 2, 4). The brick size is no longer fixed and the hardware is modified to support arbitrary bricks fetching.

7.2.10 Ineffectual Activation Skipping

For the Cnvlutin[2] accelerator, the modified dispatcher is proposed with an additional detector to skip the ineffectual activation (Figure 7.19). It first reads the activation bricks with one brick per neuron lane. It applies the comparator to detect the ineffectual activation and encodes the effectual offset in the offset vector using VIAI format. The activation valves and their offset are broadcasted to the NFU for computation. If the activation brick contains (1, 2, 0, 4), the modified dispatcher sends the (00b, 1), (01b, 2), and (11b, 4) with format (offset, value) to the NFU.

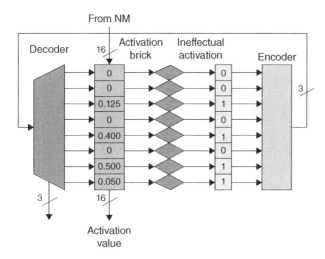

Figure 7.19 Cnvlutin[2] ineffectual activation skipping.

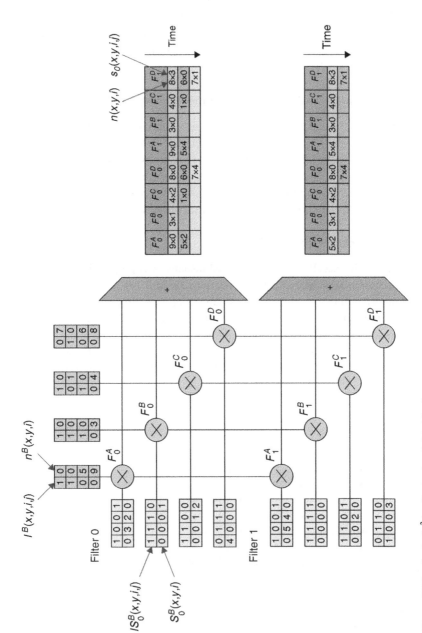

Figure 7.20 Cnvlutin[2] ineffectual weight skipping.

7.2.11 Ineffectual Weight Skipping

The Cnvlutin[2] accelerator is further modified to skip ineffectual weight. For every input activation brick n^B (x, y, i), it contains the neurons n (x, y, i) to n (x, y, i + 15). The corresponding I^B (x, y, i, j) is available with bit j indicates the activation brick is ineffectual or not. Similarly, IS^B_f (x, y, i, j) with bit j indicates the filter f with weight brick S^B_f (x, y, i) is ineffectual or not. S^B_f (x, y, i) also contains the weights from s^f (x, y, i) to s^f (x, y, i + 15). During the convolution, it skips the computation if either the activation or the weight offset is ineffectual. It speeds up the operation and reduces power dissipation (Figure 7.20).

Exercise

1 What are the design challenges for eDRAM for chip implementation?

2 How do you improve DaDianNao functional unit for layer processing?

3 How do you enhance the DaDianNao pipeline configuration for parallel processing?

4 Why is the ZFNAf format better than the CSC approach for resource utilization?

5 How do you implement the network pruning approach in Cnvlutin?

6 Can you improve the Cnvlutin brick assignment approach for data transfer?

7 Why is Cnvlutin processing order better than DaDianNao one?

8 How do you enhance the ineffectual activation/weight-skipping approach for network sparsity?

References

1 Chen, Y., Luo, T., Liu, S. et al. (2014). DaDianNao: A machine-learning supercomputer. *2014 47th Annual IEEE/ACM International Symposium on Microarchitecture,* 609–622.
2 Chen, T., Du, Z., Sun, N. et al. DianNao: A small-footprint high-throughput accelerator for ubiquitous machine-learning. *ASPLOS '14, Proceedings of the 19th*

International Conference on Architectural Support for Programming Languages and Operating Systems, 269–284.

3 Leiserson, C.E. (1985). F at-trees: Universal networks for hardware-efficient supercomputing. *IEEE Transactions on Computers* c-34 (10): 892–901.

4 Albericio, J., Judd, P., Hetherington, T. et al. (2016). Cnvlutin: Ineffectual-neuron-free deep neural network computing. *ACM/IEEE 43rd Annual International Symposium on Computer Architecture,* 1–13.

5 Judd, P., Delmas, A., Sharify, S. et al. (2017). Cnvlutin^2: Ineffectual-Activation-and-Weight-Free Deep Neural Network Computing. arXiv:1705.00125v1.

8

Network Sparsity

To eliminate the network sparsity, various approaches are proposed to skip the ineffectual zero operation to improve the system throughput. It includes the feature map encoding/indexing, the weight sharing/pruning, and quantized prediction schemes.

8.1 Energy Efficient Inference Engine (EIE)

Stanford University Energy Efficient Inference Engine (EIE) accelerator [1] supports the compressed network model for sparse matrix-vector multiplication using distributive memory and handles the weight sharing without loss of accuracy. It takes the advantage of dynamic vector sparsity, static weight sparsity, relative indexing, weight sharing, and narrow weight (four bits) to improve the throughput and reduce memory access.

EIE accelerator consists of Leading Non-Zero Detection Network (LNZD), Central Control Unit (CCU), and scalable Processing Element (PE). LNZD network detects the input sparsity. The CCU controls the network segment computation.

8.1.1 Leading Nonzero Detection (LNZD) Network

The Leading Nonzero Detection (LNZD) network supports four PEs' operations. It detects the nonzero element from the input activations and feeds them into the Leading Nonzero Detection (LNZD) node (Figure 8.1). The node broadcasts the nonzero values and its index to the PEs through separate routing.

Artificial Intelligence Hardware Design: Challenges and Solutions, First Edition.
Albert Chun Chen Liu and Oscar Ming Kin Law.
© 2021 The Institute of Electrical and Electronics Engineers, Inc. Published 2021 by John Wiley & Sons, Inc.

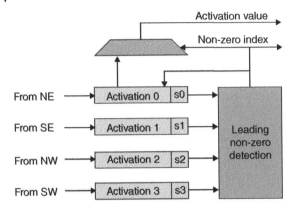

Figure 8.1 EIE leading nonzero detection network.

8.1.2 Central Control Unit (CCU)

The Central Control Unit (CCU) communicates with the host and monitors every PE state through the control register. It is divided into two operating modes, the computing and I/O modes. In computing mode, the CCU receives the nonzero input activation from distributed LNZD network and broadcasts the values to all PEs for computation. This process is repeated until all the input channels are scanned. During I/O mode, all PEs are idle, the activation and weights are accessed by Direct Memory Access (DMA) through CCU.

8.1.3 Processing Element (PE)

The PE consists of activation queue, pointer read unit, sparse matrix unit, the arithmetic unit, and activation read/write unit. During the computation, CCU broadcasts the nonzero input element and its index to the activation queue. The PE processes the input element from the head of the queue if the queue is full. The broadcast is disabled. The activation queue allows the PE to build up the backlog of work to resolve the load-balancing issue due to the nonzero elements' variation in different layers (Figure 8.2).

The pointer read unit uses the head index of the activation queue to look up the start and end pointers for the nonzero elements. To process start/end pointers in a single cycle, the pointers are stored in odd/even SRAM banks with the Least Significant Bit (LSB) for memory bank selection.

The sparse matrix read unit uses the pointers to read out the nonzero elements from the sparse matrix memory. The arithmetic unit receives the nonzero elements and performs the multiply-and-accumulate operation for the filter weights and head element of the activation queue. A bypass path is provided to route the

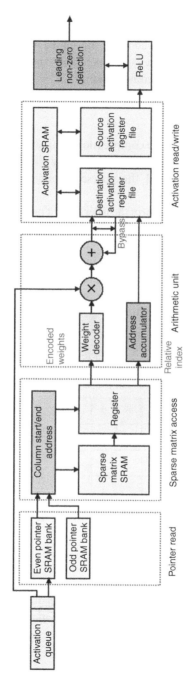

Figure 8.2 EIE processing element architecture.

output of the adder to its input if the same accumulator is used for a consecutive clock cycle.

The activation read/write unit contains the source and destination activation register files for fully connected layer operation. The role of register files is exchanged during the next layer computation.

8.1.4 Deep Compression

EIE accelerator applies the deep compression approach [2, 3] to compress the network through pruning and weight sharing. The weight below a threshold is pruned from the network and the sparse density is ranged from 4–25% (Figure 8.3).

An example shows how to perform the filter weight pruning and weight sharing with the quantization for deep compression. Assume the weight update with 4 × 4 weight matrix and 4 × 4 gradient matrix, the weight sharing replaces the filter weights with 16 possible values to four bin index and stored in the indexed table. During the update, the gradients are grouped together with the same color and multiplied by the learning rate. The filter weights subtract the corresponding scaled gradient from the shared centroids.

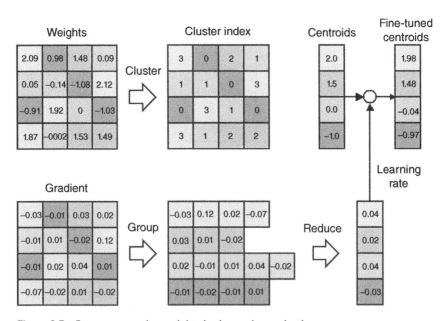

Figure 8.3 Deep compression weight sharing and quantization.

The output of the activation is defined as

$$b_i = \text{ReLU}\left(\sum_{j=0}^{n-1} W_{ij} a_j\right)$$
(8.1)

where

a_j is the input activation vector
b_i is the output activation vector
W_{ij} is the weight matrix
The equation is rewritten with deep compression

$$b_i = \text{ReLU}\left(\sum_{j \in X_i \cap Y} S\left[I_{ij}\right] a_j\right)$$
(8.2)

where

X_i is the set of column j for $W_{ij} \neq 0$
Y is the set of indices j for $a_j \neq 0$
I_{ij} is the shared weight index
S is the shared weight table

The multiply-and-accumulate operation is only performed for those columns with both W_{ij} and a_j which are nonzero.

EIE accelerator applies an interleaved Compressed Sparse Column (CSC) to encode the activation sparsity. A vector v is used to store the nonzero weights of weight matrix W, an equal length vector z encodes the number of zeros before the corresponding entry in v. Both entries v and z are stored in four bits format. If there are more than 15 zeros before the nonzero entry, an additional zero is include in the vector v. For example:

$$w = \left[0,0,1,2,0,0,0,0,0,0,0,0,0,0,0,0,0,0,0,0,0,\mathbf{0},0,0,3\right]$$
$$v = \left[1,2,0,3\right]$$
$$z = \left[2,0,15,2\right]$$

All columns v and z are stored in one large array pair with a pointer p_j points to the beginning of vector and p_{j+1} points to one beyond the last entry. Then, the number of nonzero values is given by $p_{j+1} - p_j$.

8.1.5 Sparse Matrix Computation

For sparse matrix vector multiplication, the input activation vector a multiplies with the weight matrix W to produce the output activation vector b over four PEs. It first scans the vector a to identify the nonzero element a_j and broadcasts a_j and

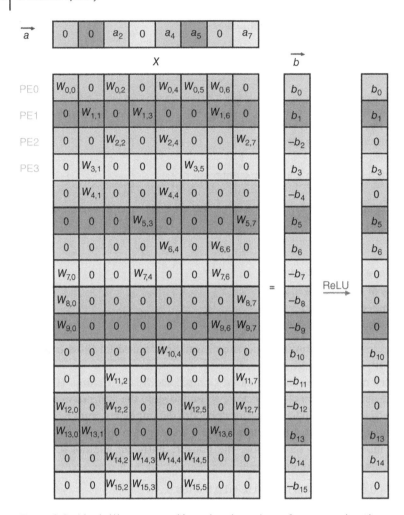

Figure 8.4 Matrix W, vector a and b are interleaved over four processing elements.

its index j to all PEs. Each PE multiplies the nonzero element a with the corresponding nonzero column elements w_j of weight matrix W, then accumulates the partial sum in an accumulator. The PE only scans the vector v with the pointer position p_j to p_{j+1} (Figures 8.4 and 8.5).

The first nonzero input activation is a_2, the values a_2 and its column index 2 is broadcasted to all PEs. Each PE multiplies a_2 by every nonzero values in column w_2

PE_0 multiplies a_2 by $w_{0,2}$ and $w_{12,2}$
PE_1 has all zero w_2 without multiplication

Virtual weight	$W_{0,0}$	$W_{8,0}$	$W_{12,0}$	$W_{4,1}$	$W_{0,2}$	$W_{12,2}$	$W_{0,4}$	$W_{4,4}$	$W_{0,5}$	$W_{12,5}$	$W_{0,6}$	$W_{8,7}$	$W_{12,7}$
Row index	0	1	0	1	0	2	0	0	0	2	0	2	0
Column pointer	0	3	4	6	6	8	10	11	13				

Figure 8.5 Matrix W layout in compressed sparse column format.

PE_2 multiplies a_2 by $w_{2,2}$ and $w_{14,2}$

PE_3 multiplies a_2 by $w_{11,2}$ and $w_{15,2}$

Then, the partial products are accumulated into corresponding row accumulators

$$b_0 = b_0 + w_{0,2} a_2$$
$$b_{12} = b_{12} + w_{12,2} a_2$$

The interleaved CSC format exploits the dynamic sparsity of activation vector a and static sparsity of weight matrix W. It allows the PEs to identify the nonzero value for multiplication. It not only speeds up the multiplication but also saves power.

8.1.6 System Performance

EIE accelerator outperforms most of CPU and mobile GPU (Figure 8.6). The results are comparable to the desktop GPU. It skips all the zero operations to speed up the overall operation. The energy efficiency is 24000 $\times$, 3400 $\times$, and 2700 $\times$ compared to CPU desktop GPU and mobile GPU with three orders of magnitude better (Figure 8.7).

8.2 Cambricon-X Accelerator

The Institute of Computing Technology (ICT), Chinese Academy of Science, Cambricon-X accelerator [4] exploits the sparsity and irregularity of the neural network model (Figure 8.8). It applies the indexing scheme to choose the nonzero neurons for parallel operations. It consists of a Control Processor (CP), a Buffer Controller (BC), an Input Neural Buffer (NBin), an Output Neural Buffer (NBout), a Direct Memory Access (DMA) Module, and Computation Unit (CU). The CP depends on the neural network model to control the BC and loads the neurons into the PEs for local computing using 16 bits fixed-point arithmetic. The critical element of Cambricon-X accelerator is the BC T_n indexing units to index the nonzero neurons for processing, the number of the indexing units is the same as the PE one.

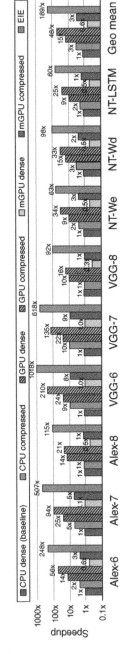

Figure 8.6 EIE timing performance comparison [1].

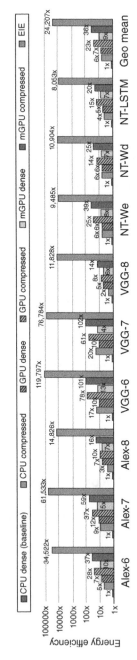

Figure 8.7 EIE energy efficient comparison [1].

Figure 8.8 Cambricon-X architecture.

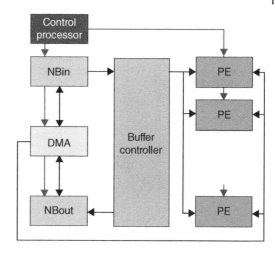

8.2.1 Computation Unit

The Computation Unit (CU) is dedicated to neural network basic operations with T_n Processing Elements (PEs). All PEs are connected using a fat tree to avoid routing congestion. Each PE consists of a PE Functional Unit (PEFU) and Synapse Buffer (SB). It reads the neurons from the BC and the synapse from the local BC, then feeds them into PEFU with two stages vector multiplication and addition pipeline for processing. The output neurons are written back to the BC. For T_n PEFU, each has T_m multiplier and adder tree. It can perform $T_n \times T_m$ multiplication-addition in parallel (Figure 8.9).

The optimal SB is designed to store synapse and minimize the memory access latency. To illustrate how to support network sparsity, seven input neurons and two output neurons are connected in a sparse neural network with four PEs (T_m = 4). The synaptic weight w_{ij} is stored in the SB which connects i^{th} input neuron with j^{th} output neuron. The weights of output neuron 0 are stored in address 0 and the weights of output neuron 1 are stored in address 1 and 2. To compute the output neuron, the SB reads once for output neuron 0 but reads twice for output neuron 1. Since the number of synapses may vary for different output neurons, it allows the SB to load the data asynchronously to improve the overall performance (Figure 8.10).

8.2.2 Buffer Controller

The Buffer Controller (BC) consists of the Indexing Module (IM) and BC Functional Unit (BCFU). The BCFU stores the neurons for indexing (Figure 8.11). It transfers the input neurons from NBin to the PE for parallel processing or

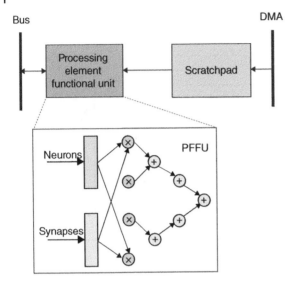

Figure 8.9 Cambricon-X processing element architecture.

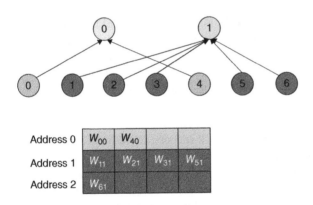

Figure 8.10 Cambricon-X sparse compression.

directly fed into the BCFU. After PE computation, the results are stored in BCFU for future processing or written back to NBout (Figure 8.12).

The IM identifies the nonzero neuron in BC and only transfers the nonzero indexed neurons for processing. There are two IM options, direct and step indexing. The direct indexing uses the binary string to indicate the corresponding synapse state, "1 for existence and 0 for absence." Each bit is added to create the accumulated string. Then, it performs the AND operation between the original and accumulated string to generate the indexed input neurons (Figure 8.13).

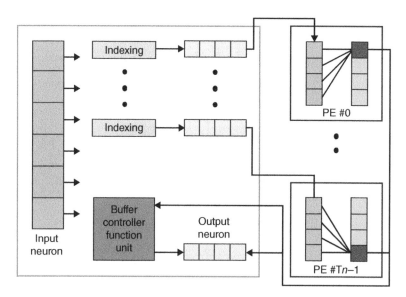

Figure 8.11 Cambricon-X buffer controller architecture.

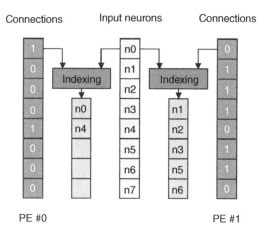

Figure 8.12 Cambricon-X index module architecture.

The step indexing uses the distance between the neurons to address the indexed input neurons. The distance in the index table is added sequentially to get the index of the input neuron (Figure 8.14).[1]

_____

1 The index of input neuron is incorrect in original paper. The correct index should be 1257 rather than 1258 (Figure 8.16).

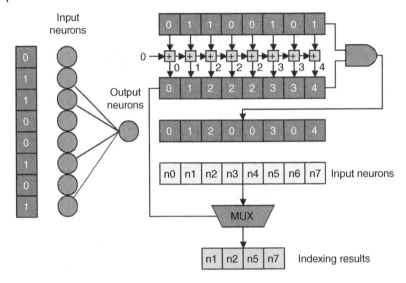

Figure 8.13 Cambricon-X direct indexing architecture.

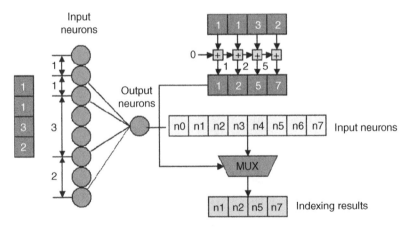

Figure 8.14 Cambricon-X step indexing architecture.

Compared between direct and step indexing approaches, the cost is increased with sparsity. The cost of step indexing is less than the direct one in terms of area and power.

8.2.3 System Performance

Compared to system performance, it is 51.55 ×, 5.20 ×, and 4.94 × faster than CPU-Caffe, GPU-Caffe, and GPU-cuBLAS with the dense network, it achieves 144.41 ×, 10.60 × improvement over CPU-sparse and GPU-sparse and 7.23 × better than DianNao accelerator (Figure 8.15 and 8.16).

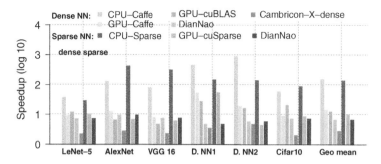

Figure 8.15 Cambricon-X timing performance comparison [4].

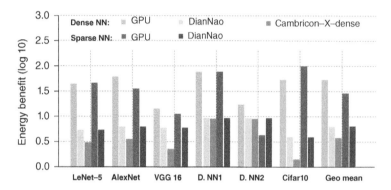

Figure 8.16 Cambricon-X energy efficiency comparison [4].

Compared to energy efficiency, it is $37.79 \times$ (dense) and $29.43 \times$ (sparse) better than the GPU, it also shows $6.43 \times$ better than the DianNao accelerator.

8.3 SCNN Accelerator

Massachusetts Institute of Technology (MIT) SCNN accelerator [5] explores both the activation and weight sparsity to eliminate the zero computation using a sparse encoding scheme. The novel Cartesian product flow is proposed for the activation and weight reuse, called Planar Tiled-Input Stationary-Cartesian Product-sparse (PT-IS-CP-sparse) flow.

8.3.1 SCNN PT-IS-CP-Dense Dataflow

The convolution is a computation-intensive operation occupied over 90% of resources. The K multiple filters $C \times R \times S$ filter weights convolute with the batch size N input activations $C \times W \times H$ to produce the output activations (Figure 8.17)

The convolution is formulated as a nested loop with seven variables (Figure 8.18):

The Planar Tiled-Input Stationary-Cartesian Product-dense (PT-IS-CP-dense) dataflow illustrates how to decompose the convolution nested loop for parallel processing. It adopts Input Stationary (IS) approach. The input activations are reused for all the filter weights' computation to generate K output channels with $W \times H$ output activations. With multiple C input channels, the loop order becomes

$$C \rightarrow W \rightarrow H \rightarrow K \rightarrow R \rightarrow S$$

The input buffer stores the input activations and filter weights for computation. The accumulator performs a read-add-write operation to accumulate all the partial sums and produce the output activations. To improve the performance, the blocking strategy is used that the K output channels are divided into K/K_c output

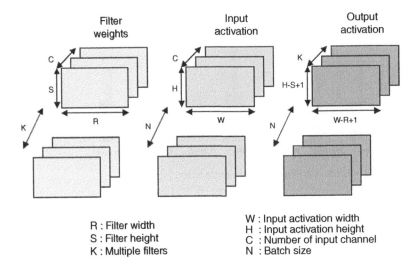

R : Filter width
S : Filter height
K : Multiple filters

W : Input activation width
H : Input activation height
C : Number of input channel
N : Batch size

Figure 8.17 SCNN convolution.

```
for n = 1 to N
  for k = 1 to K
    for c = 1 to C
      for w = 1 to W
        for h = 1 to H
          for r = 1 to R
            for s = 1 to S
              Out[n][k][w][h] + = in[n][c][w + r=1] [h + s −1] ×
                                  filter [k][c][r][s]
```

Figure 8.18 SCNN convolution nested loop.

channel groups with size K_c. It stores the filter weights and output channels in a single output channel group.

Weight $C \times K_c \times R \times S$
Input Activation $C \times W \times H$
Output Activation $K_c \times W \times H$

$$\frac{K}{K_c} \to C \to W \to H \to K_c \to R \to S$$

It also exploits the spatial reuse within the PE for intra-PE parallelism. The filter weights (F) are fetched from the weight buffer with the input activations (I) from the input activation buffer. They are delivered to the $F \times I$ array multipliers to compute Cartesian Product (CP) of the partial sums. Both filter weights and input activations are reused to reduce the data access. All partial sums are stored for further computation without any memory access.

The spatial tiling strategy is used to partition the load into a PE array for inter-PE parallelism. The $W \times H$ input activations are divided into smaller $W_t \times H_t$ Planar Tiles (PT) and distributed among the PEs. Each PE operates on its own set of filter weights and input activations to generate output activations. It also supports the multiple channels processing that $C \times W_t \times H_t$ are assigned to PEs for distributive computations.

Due to the sliding window operation, it introduces the cross-tile dependency at the tile edge. The data halos are used to solve this issue:

- Input Halos: The PE input buffer is sized up which is slightly larger than $C \times W_t \times H_t$ to accommodate the halos. It duplicates across the adjacent PEs but the outputs are local to each PE.
- Output Halos: The PE accumulation buffers are also sized up which are slightly larger than $K_c \times W_t \times H_t$ to accommodate the halos. The halos contain incomplete partial sums that are communicated with neighbor PE to complete the accumulation at the end of output channel computation.

The PT-IS-CP-dense dataflow is reformulated as follows (Figure 8.19):

8.3.2 SCNN PT-IS-CP-Sparse Dataflow

The Planar Tiled-Input Stationary-Cartesian Product-sparse (PT-IS-CP-sparse) dataflow is derived from PT-IS-CP-dense one. It supports the filter weight and input activations' sparsity. The filter weights are grouped into the compressed sparse blocks with size $K_c \times R \times S$ and the input activations are encoded with the block size $W_t \times H_t$. Similar to PT-IS-CP-dense dataflow, the PEs compute the

```
BUFFER wt_buf[C][Kc*R*S/F][F]
BUFFER in_buf[C][Wt*Ht/I][I]
BUFFER acc_buf[Kc][Wt+R-1][Ht+S-1]
BUFFER out_buf[k/Kc][Kc*Wt*Ht]
for k' = 0 to K/Kc-1                                    (A)
{
    for c = 0 to C -1
      for a = 0 to (Wt*Ht/I)-1
        {
          in[0:I-1] = in_buf[c][a][0:I-1]              (B)
          for w = 0 to (Kc*R*S/F) -1                   (C)
          {
              Wt[0:F-1] = wt_buf[c][w][0:F-1]          (D)
              parallel_for (i = 0 to I-1) x (f = 0 to F-1)   (E)
              {
                  k = Kcoord(w,f)
                  x = Xcoord(a,i,w,f)
                  y = Ycoord(a,i,w,f)
                  acc_buf[k][x][y] += in[i] x wt[f]    (F)
              }
          }
        }
    out_buf[k'][0:kc*Wt*Ht-1] = acc_buf[0:Kc-1][0:Wt-1][0Ht-1]
}
```

Figure 8.19 PT-IS-CP-dense dataflow.

cross-product of $F \times I$ partial sums where F is nonzero filter weights and I is nonzero input activations. The output index is derived from the nonzero coordinate. The accumulation buffer is modified to a distributive array of smaller accumulator buffer. The partial sums are routed into the accumulation buffer array based on its output index. The PT-IS-CP-sparse dataflow is modified to fetch the compressed sparse indexed[2] input activation (B), filter weight (D), and the accumulation buffer (F).

8.3.3 SCNN Tiled Architecture

The SCNN accelerator supports PT-IS-CP-sparse dataflow with tiled architecture. It employs a Processing Element (PE) array connected with neighbor PEs to exchange the halos. The Input Activation RAM (IARAM) received the input activations and the Output Activation RAM (OARAM) delivered the output activations (Figure 8.20). The layer sequencer controls the data movement between PE and DRAM.

---

2 Based on the PT-IS-CP-dense dataflow.

Figure 8.20 SCNN architecture.

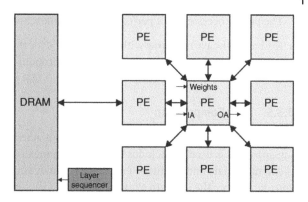

8.3.4 Processing Element Architecture

The PE consists of a weight buffer, input/output activation RAM (IARAM/OARAM), the multiplier array, a scatter crossbar, a bank of accumulation buffers and a Post-Processing Unit (PPU) (Figure 8.21). It first streams a portion of the compressed input activations and filter weights into PE. Then the multiplier array computes the Cartesian product to produce $K_c \times W_t \times H_t$ partial sums and stores in the accumulation buffer. The accumulation buffer includes the adders and a set of output channel entry. It supports a double buffer strategy, one buffer calculates the partial sum, and the other sends the outputs to PPU for post-processing.

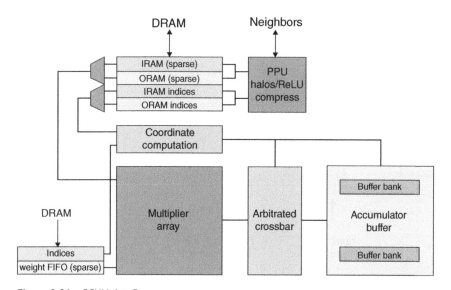

Figure 8.21 SCNN dataflow.

The post-processing unit performs several different tasks:

- Exchange the partial sums with neighbor PEs for the halo region
- Perform nonlinear activation, pooling, and dropout
- Compress the output activations and write to OARAM

8.3.5 Data Compression

To compress the filter weights and input/output activations, the modified encoding approach is used. It includes the data and index vector. The data vector stores the nonzero data and the first element of the index vector indicates the number of zero data before the nonzero element. The index vector encodes the nonzero index using four bits up to 15 zeros between two nonzero values. A zero placeholder is introduced if the number of zeros exceeds 15 without any significant compression efficiency degradation (Figure 8.22).

8.3.6 System Performance

The SCNN accelerator is compared with the dense DCNN one[3] and SCNN (oracular) design (Figure 8.23). The SCNN (oracle) design represents the upper bound for the performance. It divides the number of multiplications by 1024. The SCNN

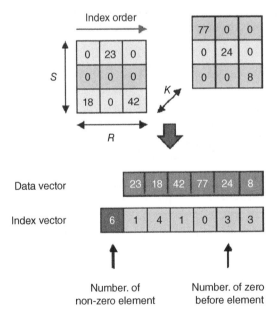

Figure 8.22 SCNN weight compression.

3 The dense DCNN accelerator is not described in detail in the paper.

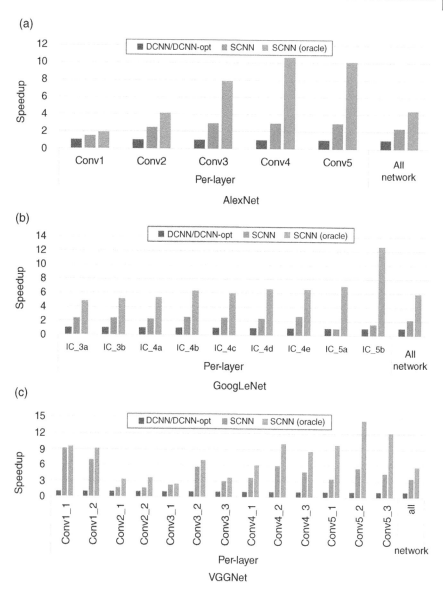

Figure 8.23 SCNN timing performance comparison [5].

accelerator outperforms the DCNN one with 2.37 ×, 2.19 × and 3.52 × using AlexNet, GoogLeNet, and VGGNet. The gap between SCNN and SCNN (oracle) designs is due to intra-PE fragmentation and inter-PE synchronization barrier (Figure 8.24).

(a)

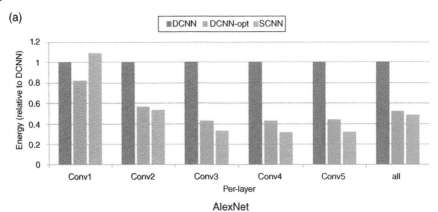

AlexNet

(b)

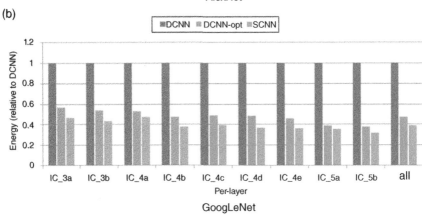

GoogLeNet

(c)

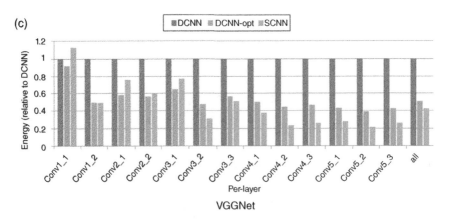

VGGNet

Figure 8.24 SCNN energy efficiency comparison [5].

Compared to the energy efficiency, the SCNN accelerator is $0.89 \times$ to $4.7 \times$ over DCNN design and $0.76 \times$ to $1.9 \times$ over DCNN-opt design dependent on the input activation density.

8.4 SeerNet Accelerator

Microsoft SeerNet accelerator [6] is proposed to predict the feature maps sparsity using quantization convolution. It applies the binary sparsity mask from the quantized feature maps to speed up the inference. The feature maps F and the filter weights W are quantized into F_q and W_q. It runs the quantized low-bit inference, Quantized Convolution (Q-Conv), and Quantized ReLU (Q-ReLU) activation to generate the sparsity mask M. Then, it performs the full precision sparse inference over W and F to create the output feature maps F' (Figure 8.25).

8.4.1 Low-Bit Quantization

Low-bit Quantization generates the quantized filter weights through online and offline operations. The complexity of quantization is only $1/(HW)$ where H and W are the output feature maps dimension. The online operation offers highly

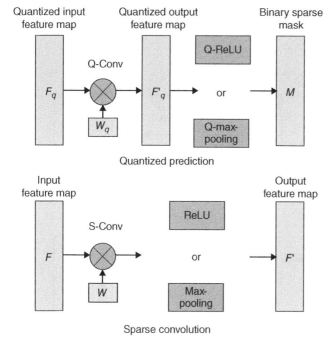

Figure 8.25 SeerNet architecture.

parallel processing with low computational complexity as well as small overhead. The offline option eliminates the quantization overhead with additional storage. During the online quantization, it runs the quantized convolution with the input features and filter weights to create a binary sparsity mask. Then, it performs the sparse convolution with the original filter weights and input feature maps to generate the output feature maps with a sparsity mask.

8.4.2 Efficient Quantization

Quantization is an effective way to speed up neural network training and inference. Instead of full quantization, it focuses on layer-by-layer quantization and applies the low-bit approach to predict the output feature maps. For ReLU activation, it only finds the sign of the output feature maps and zero out all negative values. For max pooling, it only finds the largest value in the feature maps without any precision. The low-bit quantization approach allows faster inference with less power consumption (Figure 8.26).

The quantization flow is defined as:

- Define the quantization level 2^{n-1} where $n-1$ accounts for both positive and negative ranges
- Find the max absolute value M of all tensors
- Calculate the quantized value with equation (Figure 8.27)

$$x' = \text{floor}\left(\frac{x}{M} \times 2^{n-1}\right) \tag{8.3}$$

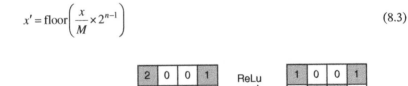

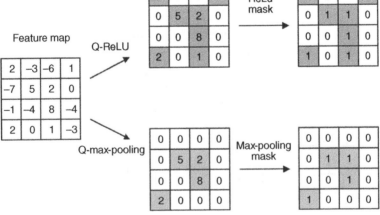

Figure 8.26 SeerNet Q-ReLU and Q-max-pooling.

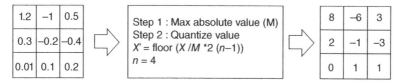

Figure 8.27 SeerNet quantization.

8.4.3 Quantized Convolution

For classical convolution

$$Y = \sum_{i}^{N} W_i \otimes X_i \qquad (8.4)$$

where

Y is the output feature maps
X_i is the input feature maps
W_i is the filter weights
$\otimes$ is the convolution operator

For integer convolution

$$f(Y) = f\left(\sum_{i}^{N} W_i \otimes X_i\right) \qquad (8.5)$$

$$f(Y) = \sum_{i}^{N} f\left(W_i \otimes X_i\right) \qquad (8.6)$$

$$f(Y) = \sum_{i}^{N} f_{w\times x}^{-1}\left(f_w(W_i) \otimes f_x(X_i)\right) \qquad (8.7)$$

where

f_x is the input feature map quantization function
f_w is the filter weight quantization function
$f_{w\times x}^{-1}$ is the dequantization function
$\otimes$ is the integer convolution

For quantized ReLU activation (Q-ReLU), it focuses on the sign only

$$\text{sign}(f(Y)) = \text{sign}\left(\sum_{i}^{N} f_{w\times x}^{-1}\left(f_w(W_i) \otimes f_x(X_i)\right)\right) \qquad (8.8)$$

$$\text{sign}\big(f(Y)\big) = \text{sign}\left(\sum_{i}^{N} f_w(W_i) \otimes f_x(X_i) \right) \tag{8.9}$$

where

sign indicates the positive or negative sign of the function

Batch normalization is used to reduce the feature maps variant shift

$$B = \frac{\alpha \times (Y - \mu)}{\sqrt{\sigma^2 + \varepsilon}} + \beta \tag{8.10}$$

If the quantized batch normalization is directly applied to Q-Conv, it introduces the errors in sparsity prediction due to quantized precision loss

$$B = \frac{\alpha \times \left(\sum_{i}^{N} W_i \otimes X_i + \text{bias} - \mu \right)}{\sqrt{\sigma^2 + \varepsilon}} + \beta \tag{8.11}$$

Apply the kernel fusion operation to minimize the quantization error

$$f(B) = f\left(\frac{\sum_{i}^{N} \alpha W \otimes X_i + \alpha (\text{bias} - \mu)}{\sqrt{\sigma^2 + \varepsilon}} + \beta \right) \tag{8.12}$$

$$f(B) = \frac{f\left(\sum_{i}^{N} \alpha W_i \otimes X_i \right) + f\left(\alpha (\text{bias} - \mu) \right)}{f\left(\sqrt{\alpha^2 + \varepsilon} \right)} + f(\beta) \tag{8.13}$$

$$f(B) = \frac{\sum_{i}^{N} f_w(\alpha W_i) \otimes f_x(X_i) + f\left(\alpha (\text{bias} - \mu) \right)}{f\left(\sqrt{\sigma^2 + \varepsilon} \right)} + f(\beta) \tag{8.14}$$

8.4.4 Inference Acceleration

In order to speed up the inference, it fully utilizes Intel AVX2 vector operations. It uses the eight bits integer operation to perform four bits arithmetic operation. With 256 bits vector operation, it can perform 32 eight bits integer operations in parallel.

8.4.5 Sparsity-Mask Encoding

It also proposes an effective encoding format to enhance the sparse convolution efficiency. It encodes the sparsity mask using the row and column index vector. It changes the feature maps into vector format. It records the sparse bit position in the column index vector and the starting position of each row column index in the row index vector (Figure 8.28).

Figure 8.28 SeerNet sparsity-mask encoding.

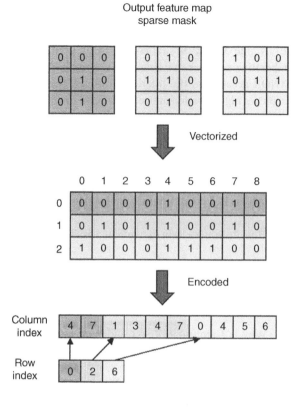

Table 8.1 SeerNet system performance comparison.

Model	Method	Top-1 accuracy drop (%)	Top-5 accuracy drop (%)	Speedup (%)	Retrain
ResNet-18	SeerNet	0.42	0.18	30.0	No
	LCCL	3.65	2.30	20.5	Yes
	BWN	8.50	6.20	50.0	Yes
	XNOR	18.10	16.00	98.3	Yes
ResNet-34	SeerNet	0.35	0.17	22.2	No
	LCCL	0.43	0.17	18.1	Yes
	PFEC	1.06	–	24.2	Yes
VGG-16	SeerNet	0.28	0.10	40.1	No
	PFEC	–	0.15	34.0	Yes

8.4.6 System Performance

The SeerNet accelerator compares with several approaches, LCCL [7], PFEC [8], BWN, and XNOR [9] (Table 8.1). LCCL predicts the sparsity through small collaborative network training. PFEC prunes the convolutional filter, BWN, and XNOR accelerates the inference through the model quantization. The SeerNet achieves higher performance improvement of 30% (ResNet-18), 22.2% (ResNet-34) and 40.1% (VGG-16) with small accuracy loss.

Exercise

1 Why is EIE deep compression good for network sparsity?

2 How do you include dynamic network pruning into EIE design?

3 How do you improve EIE processing element architecture?

4 How do you apply k-means approach for EIE network compression?

5 Why is Cambricon-X step indexing more difficult than direct indexing for implementation?

6 How do you apply SCNN PT-IS-CP-sparse dataflow for a fully connected layer?

7 How do you integrate SeerNet efficient quantization with a deep compression approach?

8 What are the advantages and disadvantages among the network sparsity approaches?

References

1 Han, S., Liu, X., Mao, H. et al. (2016). EIE: Efficient Inference Engine on Compressed Deep Neural Network. arXiv:1602.01528v2.

2 Han, S., Mao, H., and Dally, W.J. (2016). Deep compression: Compressing deep neural networks with pruning, trained quantization and huffm.n coding. In *International Conference on Learning Representations (ICLR)*.

3 Han, S., Pool, J., Tran, J. et al. (2015). Learning both Weights and Connections for Efficient Neural Networks. arXiv: 1506.02626v3.

4 Zhang, S., Du, Z., Zhang, L. et al. (2016). Cambricon-X: An accelerator for sparse neural networks. *2016 49th Annual IEEE/ACM International Symposium on Microarchitecture*, 1–12.

5 Parashar, A., Rhu, M., Mukkara, A. et al. (2017). SCNN: An Accelerator for Compressed-Sparse Convolutional Neural Network. arXiv:1708.04485v1.

6 Cao, S., Ma, L., Xiao, W. et al. (2019). SeeNet: Predicting convolutional neural network feature-map sparsity through low-bit quantization. *Conference on Computer Vision and Pattern Recognition*.

7 Dong, X., Huang, J., Yang, Y. et al. (2017). More is less: A more complicated network with less inference complexity. *Proceedings of the IEEE Conference on Computer Vision and Pattern Recognition*.

8 Li, H., Kadav, A., Durdanovic, I. et al. (2017). Pruning Filters for Efficient ConvNets. arXiv: 1608.08710v3.

9 Rastergari, M., Ordonez, V., Redmon, J. et al. (2016). XNOR-Net: ImageNet classification using binary convolutional neural networks. *European Conference on Computer Vision*.

9

3D Neural Processing

This chapter introduces the novel 3D neural processing for the deep learning accelerator. It fully utilizes the 3D Integrated Circuit (3D-IC) advantages to allow the die with the same layer function to stack together. The 3D Network Bridge (3D-NB) [1–5] provides an additional routing resource to support neural network massive interconnect and power requirements. It dissipates the heat using the Redistribution Layer (RDL) and Through Silicon Via (TSV). The Network-on-Chip (NoC) applies a high-speed link to solve the memory bottleneck. Finally, the power and clock gating techniques can be integrated into 3D-NB to support large neural network processing.

9.1 3D Integrated Circuit Architecture

3D-IC is typically divided into 2.5D interposer and 3D fully stacked architecture (Figures 9.1 and 9.2). For the 2.5D interposer design, different dies are placed on the interpose and connected using horizontal RDL and vertical TSV. NVIDIA applies this approach to solve the memory bottleneck. It connects the GPU with High Bandwidth Memory (HBM) using NVLink2 for high-speed data transfer. For 3D fully stacked design, multiple dies are stacked over each other and connected through TSV. Neurocube and Tetris accelerator adopt this configuration using Hybrid Memory Cube (HMC) to perform in-memory computation. It avoids off-chip data access to speed up the overall operation. The performance is further enhanced for NeuroStream accelerator using Smart Memory Cube (SMC). However, the cost of 3D-IC is 20% higher than Application-Specific Integrated Circuit (ASIC) which limits 3D-IC development (Figure 9.3).

  3D-IC faces two design challenges, power and thermal problems. If multiple dies are stacked together, the additional power rail is required to supply from the

Artificial Intelligence Hardware Design: Challenges and Solutions, First Edition.
Albert Chun Chen Liu and Oscar Ming Kin Law.
© 2021 The Institute of Electrical and Electronics Engineers, Inc. Published 2021
by John Wiley & Sons, Inc.

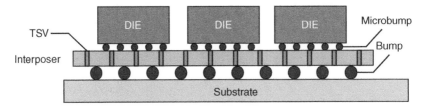

Figure 9.1 2.5D interposer architecture.

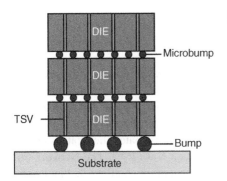

Figure 9.2 3D stacked architecture.

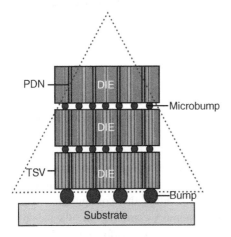

Figure 9.3 3D-IC PDN configuration (pyramid shape).

lower die to the upper one resulted in the pyramid-shaped Power Distribution Network (PDN). It occupies a large amount of routing and area. For the deep learning accelerator, the dies with the same layer functions (convolution, pooling, activation, and normalization) can't be stacked together due to different physical implementation. Stacked dies also suffer from thermal problems because the heat is difficult to dissipate from the die center. The high temperature degrades the overall performance.

To overcome 3D-IC design challenges, the RDL PDN with X topology is proposed to improve the current flow. New 3D Network Bridge (3D-NB) provides additional horizontal RDL/vertical TSV resource to solve the power and thermal issues.

9.2 Power Distribution Network

PDN is directly related with the chip performance through power rail voltage drop called IR drop. Improper PDN introduces high-resistive power rails leading to high IR drop. It degrades the overall performance. The chip may not function under the worst-case IR drop.

For chip design, the maximum IR drop is set to be 10% which translates to 10% performance degradation.

$$V_{PDN} = I_{chip}R_{PDN} \tag{9.1}$$

where

V_{PDN} is the power rail voltage drop
R_{PDN} is the power rail effective resistance
I_{chip} is the chip current

The chip voltage is expressed as

$$V_{chip} = V_{dd} - V_{PDN} \tag{9.2}$$

$$V_{chip} = V_{dd} - I_{chip}R_{PDN} \tag{9.3}$$

where

V_{chip} is the chip voltage
V_{dd} is the supply voltage

Depending on the package technology, the IR drop contour is different between wire bond and flip-chip design. For wire bond design, the power supply bumps[1] are located at the chip edge. The IR contour is concave downward where the maximum IR drop occurred at the chip center. For flip-chip design, the power supply bumps are placed at the chip center. The IR contour is concave upward where the maximum IR drop is found at the chip edge. Different PDNs are required for wire bond and flip-chip designs (Figure 9.4).

---

1 It is referred to the package power and signal bumps.

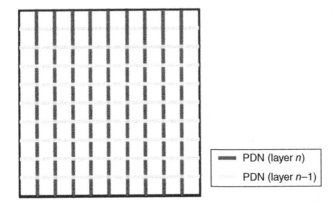

Figure 9.4 PDN – Conventional PDN Manthan geometry.

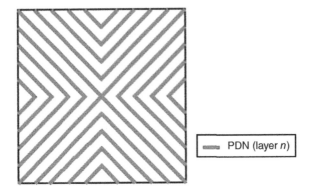

Figure 9.5 Novel PDN X topology.

The fabrication process typically offers multiple metal layers for signal routing. The narrow width/spacing low metal layer is designed for signal routing. The thick top metal layer is targeted for wire bond I/O pad to withstand the bonding of mechanical stress and also used for PDN to minimize the IR drop. PDN is configured using Manhattan topology where the top and bottom metal layers are placed orthogonally to each other. The power rails are connected using multiple vias to reduce the effective resistance. Multiple vias also help fulfill electromagnetic (EM) and Design for Yield (DFY) requirements (Figure 9.5).

For modified PDN [6–9], it replaces the top two thick metal layers with low resistive RDL and configures the power rails using the X shape. It allows the current evenly distributed over the chip for both wire bond and flip-chip designs. The X topology is recommended for top power rail but not signal routing. It obstructs the lower metal orthogonal signal routing. With the modified PDN, it can eliminate the top two thick metal power rails and reduces the 3D-IC cost almost the same as the ASIC one.

9.3 3D Network Bridge

The 3D Network Bridge (3D-NB) is derived from 3D System-in-Package (Figure 9.6). It is fabricated using mainstream technology and provides additional routing resources to resolve routing congestion. The power is distributed from the lower die to the upper one through 3D-NB horizontal RDL and vertical TSV connection and avoids the pyramid-shaped PDN design. The thermal issue is also resolved with the additional RDL/TSV routing. It acts as a cooling tube for heat dissipation.

With 3D-NB, the layer with the same function can be implemented using the same die and stacked together to support large neural network processing.

9.3.1 3D Network-on-Chip

For a deep neural network, there are massive connections between the layers. The node outputs are connected to the next layer inputs (Figure 9.7). Through the 3D Network-on-Chip (3D-NoC) approach, the node information is encapsulated in the packet and broadcasted to the network. The corresponding node fetches the packet for data processing. The 3D Network Switch (3D-NS) is also proposed to transfer the data in six different directions (East, South, West, North, Top, and Bottom). It is implemented using simple back-to-back gated inverters. The gated inverter is programmed dynamically to support various network topologies (Figure 9.8).

The network is further divided into multiple-level segments. The packet is only routed to the destination segment. The unused network is turned off to save power. It significantly reduces the network traffic and improves the overall performance. The network sparsity scheme is easy to integrate with the 3D-NoC approach (Figure 9.9).

9.3.2 Multiple-Channel High-Speed Link

Multiple-channel high-speed differential pair is used for data transfer similar to NVIDIA NVLink2 (Figure 9.10). The link runs at high speed (> 2 GHz and above) with a small magnitude. It reduces the overall power dissipation with better noise immunity. The memory controller supports a large amount of data transfer between the external memory and active logic through a multiple-channel high-speed link.

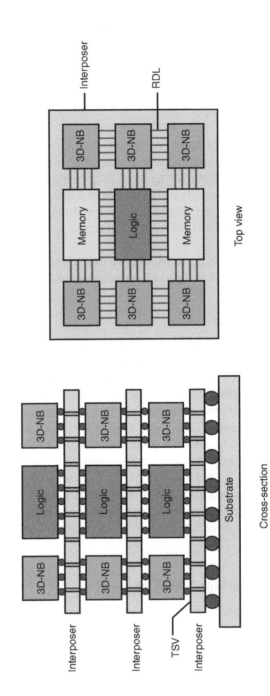

Figure 9.6 3D network bridge.

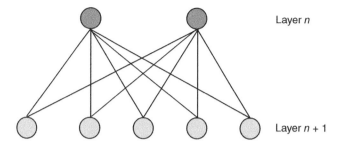

Figure 9.7 Neural network layer multiple nodes connection.

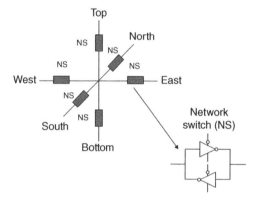

Figure 9.8 3D network switch.

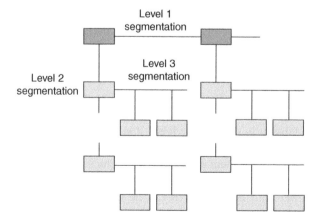

Figure 9.9 3D network bridge segmentation.

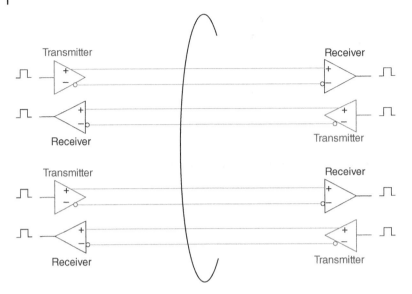

Transmitter

Receiver

Receiver

Transmitter

Transmitter

Receiver

Receiver

Transmitter

Figure 9.10 Multiple-channel bidirectional high-speed link.

9.4 Power-Saving Techniques

9.4.1 Power Gating

The two-level power gating is an effective approach to shut down the part of layers to save the power for neural network processing. The power gating separates the power rail into the global and virtual power using the power switch control. The power switch is further divided into the PMOS header switch (connected to VDD) and NMOS footer switch (connected to VSS). To reduce the area overhead, either the header or footer switch is used. The PMOS power switch is preferred over the NMOS one with less leakage and ground bounce (Figure 9.11).

The power gating partitions the active logic to multiple regions and applies the coarse-grain power gating to control the whole region power on/off. Within the region, the fine-grain power gating is used to control the particular area power on/off. If all the power switches are turned on simultaneously, it introduces voltage burst with a high in-rush current to damage the logic. It is avoided using delay logic to turn on the power switches sequentially. All the power switches and their delay logic are recommended to implement using 3D-NB to reduce the active die area overhead. 3D-NB also supports the retention flop and SRAM to preserve the logic state during the power shut down. 3D-NB can be modified to support Multiple Voltage Supplies (MVS) and Dynamic Voltage Scaling (DVS) power-saving strategies (Figure 9.12).

Figure 9.11 Power switch configuration.

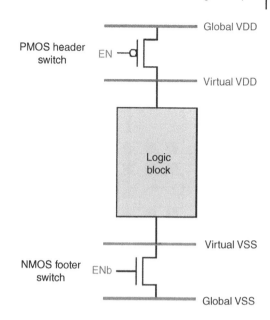

PMOS header switch

EN

Global VDD

Virtual VDD

Logic block

Virtual VSS

NMOS footer switch

ENb

Global VSS

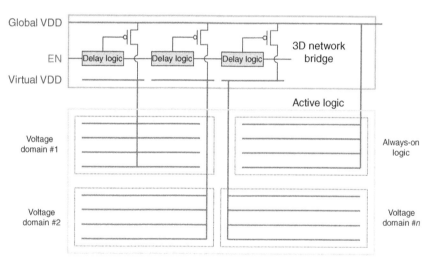

Figure 9.12 3D neural processing power gating approach.

9.4.2 Clock Gating

Neural processing is a massive parallel operation (Figure 9.13). All the operations are synchronized through the clock and the clock toggle power occupies half of the total power dissipation. It recommends the clock tree routing through 3D-NB to

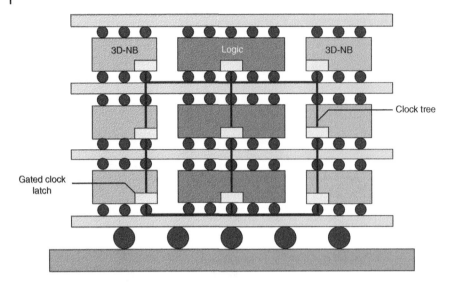

Figure 9.13 3D neural processing clock gating approach.

avoid an imbalanced clock due to routing congestion. 3D-NB also supports the clock gating with a programmable quad flop. The gated clock latch controls the clock branch on/off for power saving. The programmable quad flop groups four flops together to share the same clock input and balances the trade-off between routability and power saving. The area is typically 10–20% higher than the four individual flops but it reduces ¾ clock routing with ½ clock power saving. The quad flop is programmed to optimize the drive strength for different loading. It avoids cell swap during Engineering Change Order (ECO) to speed up the chip design.

This chapter proposes the novel 3D neural processing which is not limited to deep learning accelerator and further extends to other ASIC designs.

Exercise

1 What are three 3D-IC major challenges besides the power and thermal issues?

2 What is the 3D-IC design flow?

3 How do you design the power distribution network using a model-based approach?

4 Why is X topology not recommended for signal routing?

5 What is the basic packet format for NoC design?

6 How do you integrate the dynamic voltage-scaling approach for 3D neural processing?

7 How do you design the programmable quad flop for 3D neural processing?

8 How do you apply the 3D neural network processing approach for other design applications?

References

1 Law, O.M. and Wu, K.H. (2013). Three-dimensional system-in-package architecture. US Patent 8487444.

2 Law, O.M. and Wu, K.H. (2014). Three-dimensional integrated circuit structure having improved power and thermal management. US Patent 8674510.

3 Law, O.M. and Wu, K.H. (2015). Three-dimensional system-in-package architecture. US Patent 9099540.

4 Law, O., Liu, C.C. and Lu, J.Y. (2017). 3D integrated circuit. Patent 9666562.

5 Liu, C.C. (2019). Hybrid three-dimensional integrated circuit reconfigurable thermal aware and dynamic power gating interconnect architecture. Patent 10224310.

6 Law, O.M., Wu, K.H. and Yeh, W.-C. (2012). Supply power to integrated circuits using a grid matrix formed of through-silicon-via. US Patent US8247906B2.

7 Law, O.M. and Wu, K.H. (2013). Three-dimensional semiconductor architecture. US Patent 8552563.

8 Law, O.M., Wu, K.H. and Yeh, W.-C. (2013). Supply power to integrated circuits using a grid matrix formed of through-silicon-via. US Patent 8549460.

9 Law, O.M. and Wu, K.H. (2014). Three-dimensional semiconductor architecture. US Patent 8753939.

Appendix A: Neural Network Topology

This chapter covers different neural network topologies, it includes the popular historical configurations, Perceptron (P), Feed Forward (FF), Hopfield Network (HN), Boltzmann Machine (BM), Support Vector Machine (SVM), Convolutional Neural Network (CNN), Recurrent Neural Network (RNN).

Artificial Intelligence Hardware Design: Challenges and Solutions, First Edition.
Albert Chun Chen Liu and Oscar Ming Kin Law.
© 2021 The Institute of Electrical and Electronics Engineers, Inc. Published 2021
by John Wiley & Sons, Inc.

Neural Network Topology[1]

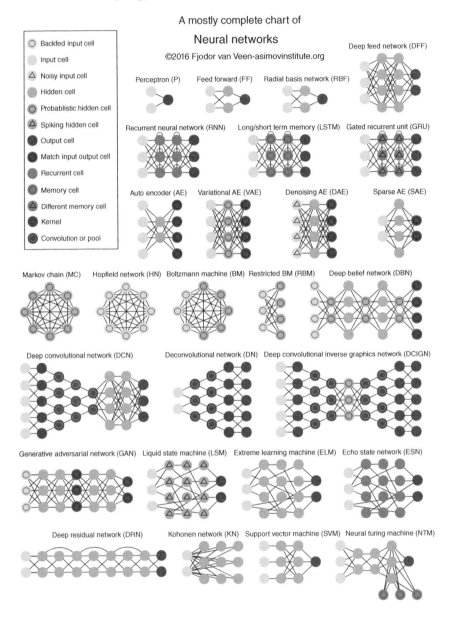

A mostly complete chart of

Neural networks

©2016 Fjodor van Veen-asimovinstitute.org

Index

Artificial Intelligence Hardware Design: Challenges and Solutions, First Edition.
Albert Chun Chen Liu and Oscar Ming Kin Law.
© 2021 The Institute of Electrical and Electronics Engineers, Inc. Published 2021
by John Wiley & Sons, Inc.